First Edition 2010

Published by: Whitman Communications
Printed in Lebanon, New Hampshire, U.S.A.

ISBN: 978-0-615-42044-8

Acknowledgements:

QLLA would like to thank the following contributors:

Deborah Doyle-Schechtman who wrote for us in 1993 a long history of the first 25 years of QLLA, a work that has been very helpful and used in shortened and edited form in this book. We recommend reading her book "By the Old Mill Stream" for a thorough, interesting and well-documented history of Quechee.

The Quechee Times editor Anne Clemens and owners Jennifer MacMillen and Sandra Smith-Ordway for giving us 30 years of Quechee Times for pictures and to review.

Frank Barrett for giving us his historical photos. We recommend reading his book "The History of Hartford" for an excellent historical account of our town.

Braxton Freeman for giving us his aerial photos.

Evelyn Taylor for her original photos of many Quechee locations.

Celebrating Quechee Lakes

A 40-Year Pictorial History

1970-2010

Produced by the Quechee Lakes
Landowners' Association

Dear Fellow Landowners:

With great pleasure the Board of Trustees and the Community Affairs Committee present *Celebrating Quechee Lakes*.

Forty years in the making, this book documents the history of this special place, its good times and bad, the happiness, sadness, friendships and memories shared by past and present members who came together to form our wonderful community.

A few years ago when Trustee Jim Keighley brought the idea of compiling a history of Quechee Lakes to the Community Affairs Committee, the Board of Trustees endorsed the idea. Sharon Taylor, with the help of Jill Tane, consented to take on the project. For over three years, Sharon, with Jill's help, worked tirelessly collecting stories and pictures, reviewing records and the *Quechee Times*, and interviewing people and publishers. While many people deserve thanks for their contributions, Sharon Taylor is the person who, more than anyone else, finally made this book happen, and for that the Quechee Lakes Landowners' Association owes her a great deal of thanks.

Additional thanks go to Deborah Doyle-Schechtman, who has graciously allowed her work on *By the Old Mill Stream*, which traces the history of the village, to be used as a reference for the early days of Quechee Lakes.

We sincerely hope you enjoy reading *Celebrating Quechee Lakes* and its walk down memory lane as you look forward to the bright future of our wonderful community.

Cordially,

The Board of Trustees and the Community Affairs Committee

Table of Contents

QUECHEE LAKES LANDOWNERS' ASSOCIATION
MISSION STATEMENT

To provide the members with a quality four season community sensitive to the natural beauty of the valley.

To meet that end, Quechee Lakes Landowners' Association endeavors to:

1) Develop and enhance the sense of community and fellowship among members.

2) Preserve the natural beauty, rural character and setting of the Valley.

3) Develop, operate and maintain a broad range of four-season amenities and activities for the benefit of our members and our guests.

4) Recognize and respond to the diversity of our membership as policies are established and implemented.

5) Constantly improve the quality of all aspects of the Association's performance.

6) Be a constructive and contributing member of our village, town and state community.

7) Preserve and enhance all of the assets of the Association and its members.

8) Manage the Association to maximize its value to its members.

9) Manage the Association's staff with challenging jobs, quality training, competitive compensation, and opportunities for personal growth in a professional environment.

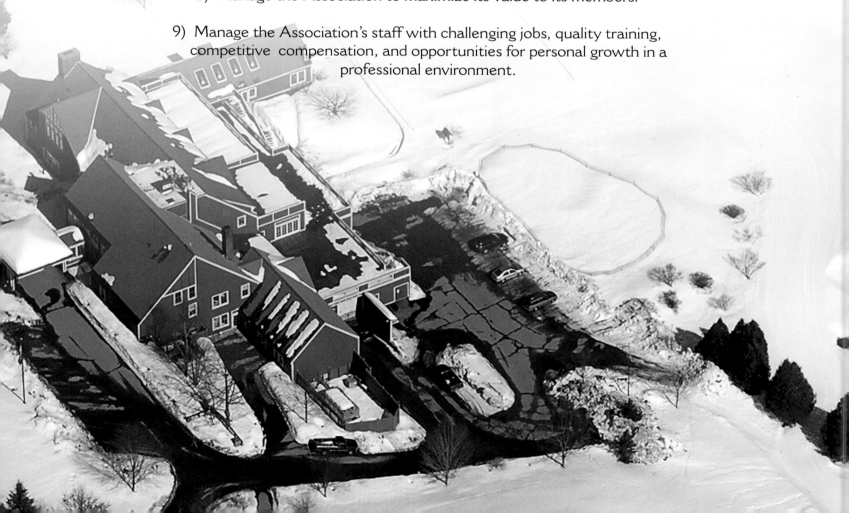

Chapter 1

The Early History of Quechee

Quechee, one of five villages in the Town of Hartford, was conceived in an atmosphere of controversy, and born during an era of land speculation.

The fracas surrounding the royal territories, and the conflicts over boundary lines separating New Hampshire from the other Land Grants issued by King Charles II of England, began in 1674. At that time, the King issued a grant to his brother James, the Duke of York, for what was to become the colony of New York. It was clearly stated in the June 29 proclamation that James' jurisdiction extended from the west side of the Connecticut River to the east side of Delaware Bay. Five years later, when Charles established the Royal Province of New Hampshire, altercations over authority ensued.

Countless boundary conflicts between Massachusetts and New Hampshire followed, and did not find resolution until 1740. The real trouble began the following year. On July 3, 1741, King George III appointed Bennington Wentworth, of Portsmouth, Governor of New Hampshire. The king commissioned him to set the western border of New Hampshire "where it meets our other governments." Wentworth interpreted his mandate as giving him license to re-define the boundary along the Connecticut River using the guidelines invoked by both Massachusetts and Connecticut when determining their perimeters. His argument rested solely on the fact that he believed New Hampshire's western boundaries were to be co-existent with those of Connecticut and Massachusetts.

Most historians agree that Wentworth's motivation was far from altruistic, because immediately after coming to this rather profitable conclusion, he not only issued his first charter, in the disputed area, but also gave it his name. The Town of Bennington, in what is now Vermont, was granted in 1749.

Governor Clinton of New York was furious and not only implored the king to remind his colleague of the stipulation in the Grant Charles II issued to James of York, but also argued the point in numerous and lengthy communications addressed to Wentworth. The two bandied the point back and forth until it was finally agreed that neither would issue grants along the western border of the Connecticut River until they received a decision from the king.

PROVINCE of NEW-HAMPSHIRE.

GEORGE the Third,

By the Grace of GOD, of Great-Britain, France and Ireland, KING, Defender of the Faith, &c.

To all Persons to whom these Presents shall come, Greeting.

KNOW ye, that We of Our special Grace, certain Knowledge, and meer Motion, for the due Encouragement of settling a *New Plantation* within our said Province, by and with the Advice of our Trusty and Well-beloved BENNING WENTWORTH, Esq; Our Governor and Commander in Chief of Our said Province of NEW-HAMPSHIRE in *New-England,* and of our COUNCIL of the said Province ; HAVE upon the Conditions and Reservations herein after made, given and granted, and by these Presents, for us, our Heirs, and Successors, do give and grant in equal Shares, unto Our loving Subjects, Inhabitants of Our said Province of *New-Hampshire,* and Our other Governments, and to their Heirs and Assigns for ever, whose Names are entred on this Grant, to be divided to and amongst them into *Sixty Eight* equal Shares, all that Tract or Parcel of Land situate, lying and being within our said Province of *New-Hampshire,* containing by Admeasurement, *Twenty Seven Thousand* Acres, which Tract is to contain *Six Miles & one half* Mile square, and no more ; out of which an Allowance is to be made for High Ways and unimprovable Lands by Rocks, Ponds, Mountains and Rivers, One Thousand and Forty Acres free, according to a Plan and Survey thereof, made by Our said Governor's Order, and returned into the Secretary's Office, and hereunto annexed, butted and bounded as follows, Viz. *Beginning at a White Pine Tree marked opposite to the South West Corner of Lebanon cross the River Connecticut, from thence North Sixty Eight degrees West Seven miles from thence from thence North Thirty four degrees East Seven miles from thence South Sixty Degrees East Six miles to a Hemlock Tree marked at the Head of Ottauquechee River falls from thence Down the River to the first Bounds mentioned*

And that the same be, and hereby is Incorporated into a Township by the Name of *Hartford* And the Inhabitants that do or shall hereafter inhabit the said Township, are hereby declared to be Enfranchized with and Intitled to all and every the Priviledges and Immunities that other Towns within Our Province by Law Exercise and Enjoy : And further, that the said Town as soon as there shall be Fifty Families resident and settled thereon, shall have the Liberty of holding *Two Fairs,* one of which shall be held on the And the other on the annually, which Fairs are not to continue longer than the respective following the said and that as soon as the said Town shall consist of Fifty Families, a Market may be

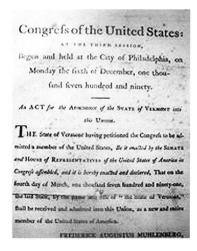

Wentworth, however, quickly broke the gentlemen's agreement he had with Clinton and continued to dole out parcels until 1754. When the war broke out between England and France, all colonization activities ceased. Those loyal to the crown during the war were to receive first priority when the land grants were resumed. Not surprisingly, Wentworth paid no heed. He saw a profit to be made in selling lots to interested parties from the lower colonies, and seized the opportunity to capitalize on the situation. Wentworth justified his radical stance by arguing that those already living in New Hampshire, loyal or not, lacked the ability to successfully cultivate the property they currently worked. He felt outsiders would be much more productive.

In keeping with that philosophy, the first renegade charters were issued and the Town of Hartford incorporated on July 5, 1761. The document awarded 27,000 acres to sixty-one individuals, requiring them to eventually pay to representatives of the province of New Hampshire one shilling per 100 acres.

When Governor Clinton of New York got wind of this he was infuriated, and immediately demanded a list of all the landowner's names west of the Connecticut. He also petitioned the king once again for a boundary decision. Wentworth, on the other hand, assured his subjects that the Governor of New York was overreacting and that the bases of his arguments were obsolete.

The king did not rule in Wentworth's favor. On July 20, 1764, the eastern bank of New York was royally declared to be the west bank of the Connecticut River, and the New Hampshire Governor was told in no uncertain terms that he no longer had jurisdiction of any of the land thereabouts, that the decree supported their assertions for control since it was established as a colony in 1674. The New York Lt. Governor, operating under his new found, royally sanctioned authority, requested, in 1766, the surrender of all pertinent New Hampshire Grants and promised a re-issue of the same under the New York seal. The real intent behind this action was not a simple paper exchange but actually a demand for re-purchase.

The colonists sent a petition for a re-grant to a council held in New York City on November 12, 1766. Oliver Willard of Hartford, Vermont, was the envoy assigned to represent the Town's 30 proprietors agent during the negotiations. The re-grant was approved, with two major stipulations. The first required that the Town of Hartford change its name to Ware, which would be part of New York's Cumberland County. The second required that each of the petitioners pay to the king their equal and fare share of all fees incurred during this process. The sum to be divided was £2,000. The towns people were up in arms over the cost of acquiring it. The figures they came up with—the price of the original Charter and surveying expenses—amounted to £192, or £3 each, a far cry from the £2,000 or £66 each demanded by New York. They didn't pay it.

The issue came up again about ten years later, and the proprietors raised the required sum by selling off approximately 1,000 acres of land. They sent the cash and the original Town Charter to New York City with Jonathan Burtch in 1772. At the April 8th council meeting, led by New York Governor William Tyron, it was agreed that the township could retain the name of Hartford and a re-grant stating such would be re-issued upon the surrender of £2,000. Burtch returned empty-handed: no money, no re-grant, no original charter, and no explanations. He was threatened with legal proceedings but they were never carried out. In fact, the issue was soon lost amidst the escalation of friction between the Colonies and the Crown.

Once the war with Great Britain was over and the Colonies gained their independence, the people of the New Hampshire Land Grants west of the Connecticut River declared their territory to be an independent state and vowed to assist their brethren in a newly formed United States of America against tyrannical invasion. They did so, however, as a republic, because the 1777 Continental Congress recognized New York's claim on the area. For fourteen years Vermont, briefly known as New Connecticut, ruled independently, passing its own policies, minting its own coins, and issuing its own currency. It did not join the Union until March of 1791.

The area known as Quechee Village grew out of the second Hartford Land Grant Division. The acreage, referred to as the Waterqueechee Lots, was issued in 1768. The lots were so named for the body of water they flanked, a river listed on the 1775 map of the area as Waterqueihey River, or Quatackqueohe. The name may be inherently aboriginal for "a swift mountain stream" or the word comes from the Celtic for "chasm." The river has been listed as Quarterquechee, Water Quechee, Waterqueihey, Quataqueoke, Ottaqueechy, Ottaquechee, Queechee, and finally as it is currently known, Ottauquechee. The village's official spelling, Quechee, was set by the U.S. Postal Service in March 1868.

People from "away" did in fact become the Town Proprietors, and perhaps the most famous and influential of these well heeled pioneers was Colonel Joseph Marsh. The Marsh family has influenced not only the village and the town, but some of its members perceptions and actions shaped the thinking of the state and the nation.

Colonel Joseph arrived at the mouth of the White River amidst the Land Grant controversies in 1772, along with two brothers, two cousins, a widowed mother and ten of his 12 children. Between Joseph and his brother Able, the two Marshs owned almost all of the land along the north side of the Ottauquechee in what was to become known as the Village of Quechee.

In 1776, he was commissioned Colonel in command of the Upper Regiment of Cumberland County. The following year he was a member of the convention in which "New Connecticut" declared its independence and changed its name to Vermont. He was also part of the 1777 Convention that reviewed and adopted the state constitution. This document was the first of its kind to prohibit slavery and to grant universal manhood suffrage. In 1778, he was appointed Vermont's first Lieutenant Governor serving under Governor Thomas Chittenden. Marsh held the post again the following year, when the state motto, "Freedom and Unity," was assumed, and again, from 1787-1789.

Colonel Joseph Marsh's political offices also included: Hartford Representative to the General Assembly, Chief Judge of Windsor

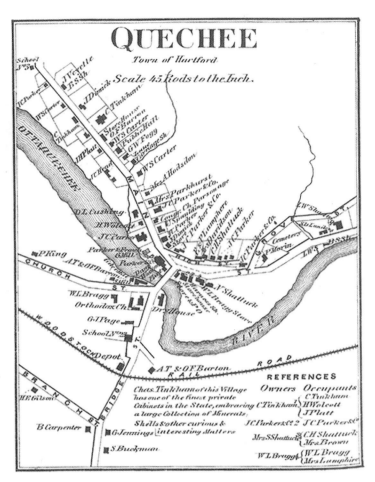

The Quechee Times published its first article in 1872 but did not publish continuously until one hundred years later in 1972, when John Davidson announced its reestablishment. Since that time it has been providing news of the village and the people and businesses in and around Quechee Lakes.

Colonel Joseph Marsh's home, known as the Baronial Mansion

County, Chairman for the Committee on Safety, Chairman of the Court of Confiscation for Eastern Vermont, and Council Censor.

In 1793, at the age of sixty-seven, Marsh built a home "...opposite where the Quechee River breaks into little islands." Once completed, the Georgian style home was referred to by the locals as the Baronial Mansion. Marsh conducted all of his business from his new home, including overseeing the sawmill, gristmills, and fulling mills erected near the falls. Quechee became known as a mill town, as well as a home for the landed gentry.

Marsh's wife, Dorothy Mason Marsh, was a direct descendent of Charlemagne, Alfred-the-Great, and Henry VIII, as well as several other sovereigns of Europe. Their son Charles was appointed district Attorney of Vermont by President George Washington in 1797, was a member of the U.S. Congress and a Trustee of Dartmouth College. Their youngest son, William, was a pioneer in the anti-slavery movement and was reported to have donated $25,000 during his lifetime to further the cause.

The accomplishments of Dorothy and Joseph's grandchildren were equally impressive. Charles' son, George Perkins Marsh, has been deemed "the father of the American ecological movement." Daniel's son, James, is credited with having introduced Transcendental thought to America, and was the University of Vermont's fifth

president. His brother Leonard was an author, scholar, physician and professor. Many of the works he penned challenged the institution of slavery.

Another prominent resident of the village, and as it happens, owner of Marshland from 1846-1901, was the Honorable John Porter. He was, during his life in Quechee: one of the original stockholders in the Woodstock Railroad; President of the Ottauquechee Savings Bank; Director of the Vermont/Canada Railroad; member of both the state Legislature and Senate; Director of the Vermont State Prison; Commissioner to prepare and erect the State Capitol in Montpelier after a fire destroyed the existing one in 1857; and Probate Court Judge. The latter position he held for thirty-six years.

Mill owner, A.G. Dewey, though involved in Quechee affairs, resided in the adjacent hamlet of Dewey's Mills. Dewey and his family not only revolutionized the American wool industry, but also served their state in a number of civic and political capacities.

Quechee was also home to Andrew Tracy, a lawyer and judge; William Strong, a Congressman, Supreme Court Judge, and Sheriff; Vermont Secretary of State Charles Porter; numerous members of the General Assembly and the State Senate, and a host of successful and not so successful mill owners and farmers.

Chapter 2

The Rise and Fall of the Mill Towns

Early town proprietors saw the value of river land. They envisioned mills bringing jobs. By 1774 the town conveyed land to John Marsh providing he establish saw and grist mills. Completion of a saw mill, grist mill, and wool fulfilling mill in the Quechee village center and erection of a bridge made Quechee the most important village in the township of Hartford. For four decades, 1771-1811, immigration increased the population.

In 1825, John Downer and Company built a six-story structure out of bricks believed to have come from the vicinity of what is now the Quechee Club, once the site of the Udall brickyard. John Downer's business failed the first year and the old Downer Mill on Main Street that John Downer built changed hands many times before being purchased by two gentlemen, J. C. Parker and Denison Taft, from Barre, in 1857. J.C. Parker and Co. put the troubled woolen mill back on its feet.

Above: *Mill women workers c. 1900*

As farming trends changed and people were raising sheep as their primary livestock, the mills in Quechee flourished. Everyone was involved at least on the subsistence level, and the early mills supported them. The gristmills ground their grain, the fulling mills processed their wool, and the sawmill planed their timber. In 1870, the Quechee mill was one of 45 such plants contributing 35% of the 3.5 million dollar revenue the state woolen industry generated that year. Parker's business, and that of A.G. Dewey, were greatly enhanced by the Woodstock Railroad which became totally operational in 1875. J.C. Parker and Co. produced some of the finest white baby flannel, material used to make petticoats, men's shirts and pajamas.

The Quechee mill utilized both water and horsepower to operate 26 looms, 28 card sets, and one elevator. The business employed 45 people in 1870, and produced approximately 100 yards of fabric a day. In 1888, 75 people were employed and the daily yield was 1500 yards per day. The economy of the village was booming. Residents supported three general merchandise stores, a horse and blanket manufacturer; a harness maker and dealer; two blacksmiths; and it required the services of a saw mill, a shingle mill, a grist mill, a cider mill, a church, a post office, and two schools.

Above and Right:
The Quechee Mill

The wool market in Vermont, however, began to decline due to the lowering of the Protective Tariff in the 1840s, and from the western competition generated by the railroad. Farmers and mill owners scrambled, in different directions, to stay in business.

In 1868, the Vermont Board of Agriculture began extolling the merits of dairy farming. The availability of light machinery during this period ensured a manageable harvest for cutting hay. Local growers began tending dairy herds, raising the fodder to feed them, and selling their milk, cheese and butter to major creameries. Sheep barns were turned into hay barns, and wheat, rye and oats swayed in the meadows where the lambs once grazed.

The first dairy association in the United States was founded in Vermont in 1869. By the 1880s, creameries sprang up in the east central part of the state. Farmers were paid for their cream content and sent home with skim milk to feed their stock. By 1890, the farming transition was virtually complete. Vermont was now a full-fledged dairy state, and the pastures around Quechee were dotted with Jerseys.

A second mill was built by the A. G. Dewey Company over a 30-foot waterfall. The mill produced 1300 yards of cloth per day and the J. C. Parker Mill, even after the devastating flood of 1869, was producing 30000 yards of quality flannel a year and employing 50 people.

Down the road in Dewey's Mills, life was good. Producing a different type of wool, "shoddy", it boasted over sixty buildings. These included a post office, family dwellings, boarding houses, a company store, mill buildings and storage sheds covering 1400 acres. It was a patriarchal community with low rents, garden plots available, a baseball field and more. Dewey's Mills had the largest payroll in the town of Hartford.

A. G. DEWEY
1805-1886

Opposite: *The Dewey's Mills complex*

Below: *Dewey's Mills employees - 1944*

Nearly six thousand people were employed in Vermont's mills built in the late 19th century. They were floundering in the mid-twentieth century as woolen mills in New England were dying out. Vermont's mills relied heavily on overflow from the larger New Hampshire and Massachusetts mills. J.C. Parker continued to operate the mill with different partners including Dewey and William Lindsay until Harris, Emery Company bought the mill in 1908.

In 1875, the railroad linked Woodstock and Quechee with White River Junction which had become one of the premier rail transportation centers in New England, but the rise of the automobile resulted in the last run of the Woodstock railroad in April 1933 and the railbed became the main road.

Top: The Quechee bridge road became part of the new highway and car traffic became common through the village in the mid-twentieth century.

Above: *The Woodstock Railroad*

Times were difficult for Quechee's mills in 1930s due to numerous factors—the depression, inexpensive textile mills abroad and the growth of the synthetic industry. The Harris-Emery Mill closed after a workers' strike in 1951 and Dewey's Mill at the head of the gorge closed in 1958 when the federal government built a flood control dam downstream. Since it was a potential flood plain, the entire site was condemned by the Army Corps of Engineers and the mill and workers' homes were destroyed. Quechee now had a large vacant building in the heart of the village. Windows were broken and streets were littered. Most of the homes were not well maintained and with the rapid decline, people moved away in the 1960s.

In 1964 the three most easterly sections of the mill on Quechee's Main Street were actually blown up after being deemed a safety hazard. The Quechee historic mill district was restored beginning in 1969 and was listed on the National Register of Historic Places on July 3, 1997.

Above: The Quechee Mill

Above Left: "Rats, trash, poverty, and welfare cases were the order of the day when a New England textile village has its one prime industry close down." – L. John Davidson about Quechee

Left: Dewey's Mills 1962

Chapter 3

Quechee Lakes — The John Davidson Era

John Davidson

L. John Davidson was born in Andover, Massachusetts. The son of a local shopkeeper and restaurateur, he attended Andover Academy and Harvard University before enlisting in the U.S. Air Force. Upon leaving the service in 1956, John as he puts it, "became interested in the real estate business because of very strange things that were happening in Andover at that time."

Davidson's hometown was the first in the country scheduled to undergo urban renewal. The plans called for the town square to be converted into a type of strip mall, an idea that did not sit well with Davidson. He combined forces with another merchant in town, Phidias Dantos, a childhood acquaintance whose family business lay at the opposite end of Main Street. Together, Davidson figured they knew almost everyone in Andover. They worked side by side for almost two years trying to glean support against the proposed strip development. They prevailed and the project was turned over to these two young men. They formed a company called Danton, and over the next five years "remodeled about every building on Main Street," Davidson said.

Dantos and Davidson had been talking about doing some sort of residential development on Cape Cod according to Dantos, and in 1966 Davidson and Louis Kane were discussing possibilities in northern New England. Davidson, still maintaining his interest in Danton, formed a separate partnership with Kane to pursue a vision they shared for a multi-dimensional environment which incorporated rural New England living. Their basic premise embraced local traditions and celebrated the area's natural resources, but it was clearly, at this stage, simply a vision. Finding an appropriate location would absorb the better part of a year. Kane and Davidson spent every available weekend driving around Maine, New Hampshire, and Vermont searching for the ideal picturesque location.

Conversations around the development in Vermont continued, Kane had become a third partner in Danton (in 1966). Arthur Contas of the Boston Consulting Group, and an Andover classmate of Davidson's, expressed an interest as did Kane's lawyer and friend, Arthur Blasenberg, of the legal firm known as Sullivan and Worcester. It was Blasenberg who introduced his childhood friend, Hollis Sheridan Paige, to the group. Paige when asked by Blasenberg if he would have any interest in the Vermont project was intrigued and was then encouraged to meet with Davidson. He arrived in Andover in the fall of 1967 and spoke to Davidson and Dantos. Paige left for the Green Mountains the very next day armed with a sheaf of U.S. Geological survey maps. It should be made clear that Paige headed for Vermont but not a specific place in Vermont. His only real mandate was to find a location that would be conducive to building a lake, because both Davidson and Kaine felt strongly that the added dimension of water was crucial to the success of their plan.

A study, commissioned by Henry T. Bourne, head of the Woodstock Planning

L. JOHN DAVIDSON (right), chairman of the board, and Quechee Lakes President Donald H. Vance, discuss their progress in turning 6000 acres of Vermont into a community that offers both recreational amenities and quiet country living in a setting that endeavors to place man-made facilities in less conspicuous sites and keep the fields open. Restoration of early Vermont farmhouses is part of the program.

MAIN St. QUECHEE Vt. 16.

Commission, financed by Laurance Rockefeller and sanctioned by Governor Hoff, had targeted the Quechee area to become the country's 27th Beautification Project. The study, the Kiley Report, written by Dan Kiley in February of 1967, proposed investigating the site for outdoor recreational capabilities while identifying ways to preserve the Vermont rural scene. On September 18, 1967, the organizational meeting of the Quechee Advisory Council to the Ottauquechee Valley Regional Planning Commission was held. Village residents believed that efforts should be made to develop tourist attractions and promote outdoor activities to vacationers and over half of the respondents thought that a recreational and tourist-related industry would bring relief to the economy. They chose village renewal as their number one priority for development. When asked if they would consider "outside" help in achieving their goals, over 71% voted yes.

The Kiley Report is believed to have influenced the identification of the Quechee site. Unanimously agreed upon, Paige and Davidson began negotiations with the townspeople, the selectmen and village landowners. The developers made no secret of their intent. The men spent months visiting with individuals in their homes, in their barns, and out in their fields, obtaining options on the coveted property, if not the property itself. Davidson, Kane, and Paige initially purchased the local properties under their own names, with financial backing obtained through the partnership

Kane and Davidson had formed for this express purpose. The 2.25 million dollars committed from various Boston banks provided them with the necessary capital to operate in this manner until the Quechee Lakes Corporation (QLC) was registered in Delaware in the spring of 1968.

In 1969, over 2,000 acres were secured, with options, or right of first refusal, on over 1,000 additional acres. This figure grew to 5500, by 1971, resulting in QLC's claim to nearly a quarter of the land in the Town of Hartford. With such a vast amount of acreage at their disposal, QLC was able to create amenities—golf courses, ski hills, lakes and tennis courts—and to build enough homes to support them. The completion of Interstates 91 and 89 also provided the development with direct access to major cities. The dream fast became a reality, and in turn, the largest development of its kind in New England.

Renovations of the historic houses in the center of the village were important to Davidson. One hundred thousand dollars was spent reclaiming the Parker House alone and nearly a million dollars went into preserving the other structures along Main Street and the banks of the Ottauquechee.

When John Davidson had completed building the Village Green according to their plan, they had moved a great deal of dirt and put in the road. The construction resulted in dirt blowing through Main Street coating the buildings there. A "painting bee" was Quechee residents' answer to cleaning up Main Street. Many volunteers gathered and spent the weekend cleaning and painting all the properties with white paint.

The Quechee bridge's first known span was in 1769 when Captain Abel Marsh was selected to oversee the project near his family's sawmill. The area where it crosses the river was known as Pinneo's Point and believed to be named after Daniel Pinneo a commissioner and constable of highways in the late eighteenth century. The bridge fell into disrepair three decades after it was built and was replaced by the town in 1803 and rebuilt again in 1885 and lost in 1933 probably due to flood damage sustained in 1927. It was an odd design because of the lattice work on one side while the other was tightly boarded. It was thought that the side facing the mill and falls was lattice work so those crossing in their wagons could look out over the falls.

In 1969, the Corporation commissioned Charles Hood Helmer of Woodstock, Vermont, to create a wooden structure to cap the bridge. The only criteria Helmer was given were that it must contain open structural work, viewing windows for children, and pedestrian walks. The revitalized bridge was dedicated in May 1970.

Above: the Quechee Bridge

Above: The Painting Bee

When John Davidson's crew moved large amounts of dirt to create the Village Green, many of the structures on Main Street were damaged, so the Quechee residents got together and had a painting bee to repaint the homes.

Chapter 3

John Davidson's Master Plan in His Own Words

The following is quoted and edited from a letter mailed to the District Environmental Commission IX from the Quechee Lakes Corporation on June 17, 1971 by L. John Davidson:

HISTORY and SCOPE

To understand the program at Quechee, we consider it desirable to develop the historical presence of the Corporation. Quechee Lakes Corporation was conceived of by L. John Davidson and Louis 1. Kane in 1964. They joined together under the proposition that no development in Northern New England was doing a job worthy of their consideration to live in. A whole environment was not being offered and a theme indigenous to New England was absent. It was felt that a project should represent a whole scope of living, and, if it were done properly, would include the traditions, scenery, and many faceted benefits of rural New England Living.

In 1966 the Ottauquechee Regional Planning Commission, headed by Henry T. Bourne had undertaken a study of the whole Ottauquechee Valley. This report was done for the agency by Daniel Kiley, a responsible land planner whose offices are located in Vermont. The report subsequently was referred to as the Kiley Report. Within that report, the Valley, approximately thirty miles in length, was looked at from a highest and best use point of view for people, their needs, and a balance of those needs with serious attention to environmental preservation. Mr. Bourne heard of our desire to locate somewhere in the Ottauquechee Watershed, and, with the recommendations of the Kiley Report in mind, recommended that we look into the valley around Quechee Village.

At first glance the sight was frightening. It was a typical, if not classic, illustration of what happens to a New England textile village when the one prime industry fails. Rats, trash, poverty and welfare cases were the order of day at the Village Center. In the beautiful hills surrounding the village, 50% of the farms had from five to twenty year growth on their unattended pastures. The residual farmers were hard-pressed between higher labor costs, the necessity for larger herds, higher feed costs, and historically inadequate milk prices.

The first impression was additionally frightening, knowing that we had to deal with up to 100 landowners, and, not only were we faced with the problem of the simplest business decision as to whether or not we would be successful in marketing the highest quality project of its nature in New England, but we were faced also with the additional problem of not being able to secure enough of the property to guarantee the environment and the ability to do a project of the scope that we felt was necessary.

Beyond the liabilities and risks that we understood to be present, we felt that Quechee and its Valley had great potential. Before committing wholly to locating in Quechee, we felt that it was appropriate to talk to the selectmen of the Town of Hartford as well as with the appropriate State Agencies. The Town of Hartford accepted our statements of intent and descriptions on standards of face value, Without their honest approach to our proposition at that time, this significant contribution to the Town's well-being would never have been possible. Similarly, Governor Philip Hoff received us with commissioners or representatives from each State Agency at a meeting twice during the initial period.He, too, allowed that if our standards were as we described, he saw no problem with our coming to the State, and, in fact, recognized the economic benefit to the community and to Vermont. Contingent upon the degree of responsibility we showed from that point forward he assured us in the presence of the members from the other Agencies that the State's cooperation would be available. Contingent upon the degree of responsibility we showed from that point forward he assured us in the presence of the members from the other Agencies that the State's cooperation would be available. Subsequently, Governor Deane Davis succeeded Governor Hoff, and we similarly made a presentation to him and the Agencies. We received in substance a similar reception to our ideas, which, at that point, had progressed to the point of commitment in several instances of acquisition. Our Land Plan still on display in our...

offices, dated...October, 1969, prepared by Sasaki, Dawson and DeMay and Associates, resulting from two years of study prior to that date, expresses exactly the same plan in general concept of product and land use as the submission to you today. The original scope of the project, which remains unchanged, was to acquire around 6,000 acres as contiguously as possibly within the natural Valley of Quechee. Within that framework we felt that we would concentrate on existing blight within the Village, restore those features within the Village that had historical significance, beautify the whole Village area regardless of ownership, and in a general sense add the dimension of pride in property, aesthetic beauty and historical interest as an end product.

Our next step was to consider what outside of the Village gave it its Vermont beauty. It became clear to us that the barns and farms, the pasture land and the fence rows were the significant contributors to this "Vermont Look." Obviously our Land Plan had to accommodate the preservations, and, in fact, reversal of the trend that had already allowed 50% of the land to grow over into woodlands. The third consideration was to create enough amenities within the Valley to attract enough people with modern desires to come to the Valley in enough quantities to make the project economically feasible. All this to be done within the framework of not losing any ground in any respect on the basic charm of the Valley. The Corporation currently owns approximately 5,500 acres.

Using precisely 6,000 acres as the key determination of all formulas within the Plan, the Corporation intends to do the following:

1. Create 2,000 home sites.
2. Create 500 living units in Condominium ownership.

The above consideration means that the Corporation intends to create one single family lot per 3 acres owned, plus one condominium living unit per 12 acres owned.

The residual acreage, nearly half of the 6,000 acres, would be used as Common Land. This Common Land does many things for all the people including those outside of the project. It is our method of preserving the aesthetic considerations of Vermont. It is our method to consider key wildlife areas. It is our method of providing compatible amenities within the countryside. To wit: stables in the existing barns. Golf courses on the existing pasture lands. Lakes along the valley floor. Wildlife areas as applied for at Deweys Mills.

Our Plan does not include building along existing Town roads except in rare instances, for we felt it was important that for as long as is possible the rural character of these roads will remain the same long after we have gone. The Corporation uses existing Town roads as access only to its own roads that it is building to Town specifications and, effectively, no frontage at all along the road by the lot.

Once the town planning commission and the developer agreed on the basic ingredients of the whole plan, then occurred, in fact, a two-way guarantee. The town would be guaranteed that the developer could proceed in following a master and with his charted course on record with them. The developer would be guaranteed that he would not be caught half way by changes in zoning or changes in personnel on the commission or innumerable variances that would be necessitated from existing by-laws that did not have the flexibility within them to accommodate such needs. The Town of Hartford was the first town in the State to adopt the by-laws as a result of the 1968 act. This Corporation had submitted its Master Plan to the Town and had received its approval. The Corporation has effectively submitted to the Town four sections of its development illustrated as numbers one through four on the Master Plan submitted to you, as well as the over-all concept philosophy including the density described herein and including the commercial areas along with other amenities also described on the Plan submitted to you. Prior to Act 250 the Corporation created two subdivisions, number two and four, and subsequently has submitted applications for numbers one and three as well as the Lake at Dewey's Mills.

FINANCIAL RESPONSIBILITY
It was outlined earlier that Quechee Lakes Corporation was formed by Louis I. Kane and L. John Davidson. It became a formal entity in 1967. Subsequent to that time, Davidson and Kane merged their other independent activities into the one entity of Kane Financial Corporation, located in Boston, Massachusetts. In 1969, the CNA Financial Corporation approached Kane Financial Corporation with the proposition of becoming a wholly owned subsidiary of CNA Financial

Corporation. CNA Financial Corporation was a holding company based in Chicago whose origins stemmed from primarily two insurance companies. These were Continental Casualty and Continental Assurance. The holding company is ranked as Americas 51st largest corporation with approximately 3.5 billion dollars in assets. Kane Financial Corporation decided to become a subsidiary of CNA, and therefore, their ownership in Quechee Lakes Corporation was transferred to the parent. As a result, CNA Financial Corporation owns 100% of Kane Financial Corporation which in turn owns 87% of Quechee Lakes Corporation.

One of the prime considerations in the decision to make Quechee effectively a subsidiary of CNA was that, although the project and its finances had been accomplished along with a significant portion of the land and marketing planning, it was felt that CNA's credibility for follow through might become an important consideration for potential customers as well as to Local and State Agencies. After a decision was made, we found the high standards CNA wants from the project as a model of what can be done, as well as their in-fact support, did create customer confidence that a Corporation of such size must mean what it says.

PROJECT STATUS

The Plan submitted to you includes the 5, 500 acres mentioned. The colored areas show definitive thinking of approximately 2,200 acres as represented by those subdivisions existent, under construction, or under application. The two proposed lakes are shown. One of which has had its final hearing by the Water Resources Board. The 18 holes of golf are either existent or under construction, The ski area is existent. One pond within the golf course is existent. Deeds are being prepared of the Common Land areas to be recorded under the name of Quechee Lakes Landowner's Association, Inc. Proposed trails and arterial roads are outlined throughout the project. The overall density represented to the Town is to be exactly what has been stated in this application. Approximately half of the condominiums are represented in the areas indicated on this first phase because that nature of product is more amenable to the inner regions.

In certain other instances we are experimenting with single family homes but owned in a condominium entity. In no instance is open land sold except in a farmstead, and, even then, restrictions on house styles, location of the homes in terms of building massing or inside or outside of a tree - line are carefully considered.

ECONOMIC IMPACT

We expect that 2,500 families and their guests, all of which will be more or less affluent, will spend locally $15,000,000 per annum. This has to be more jobs and more per capita income than currently exists. Currently, the Quechee Lakes Corporation directly or indirectly is contributing the equivalent of the total paycheck to 100 people in the area. For two consecutive years the Town tax ratio has gone down. This is an unusual set of circumstances most anywhere else.

SOCIAL IMPACT

Act 250 deals with, in a general sense, the well-being of the people of the State. We have covered the topic of jobs and income. The feeling of pride in their Town has been re-injected in Quechee. To wit: The number of families that are cleaning up their properties by themselves. Children are enjoying our ski hill. As soon as our pond is built they will be enjoying a swimming place in Quechee for the first time. We are building a playground. On our Plan we have reserved land without cost already for an additional church, for future police and fire substations, a school site, or whatever else the Town might decide to do this those areas. In no way could anyone deny that there has been a general upgrading emotionally and aesthetically to the people of the community. Not only is there evidence of pride, but also of prosperity and confidence in the future.

Your kind and prompt consideration to this request is both needed and solicited.

Very Truly Yours,

L. John Davidson
Chairnan of the Board of Directors
Chief Executive Officer
Quechee Lakes Corporation
UP/cr
Enclosures

Chapter 4

Quechee Lakes Landowners' Association is Founded

On February 19, 1970, in the White River Junction, Vermont Municipal Building offices of Black and Plante, the Incorporators of the Quechee Lakes Landowners' Association (QLLA) held their first meeting. Hollis S. Paige, Raffael Terino and Peter Plante gathered to file the following Articles of Association:

1. To hold, manage and regulate and maintain certain common areas, trails, paths, roads, parking areas, swimming facilities, beaches, docking area, ski area, golf course, core community clubhouse facility together with other facilities to be used in common by all owners of lots and condominiums, and said owners of said lots shall be subject to and abide by all laws, rules and regulations of the Association governing said use.
2. To set dues and certain use fees and other such miscellaneous fees as to be determined.
3. To provide the owners of property in the Quechee Lakes Development with a voting right as to the use and operation of the facilities in the Development.
4. All other purposes as may be necessary to carry out these aims.

The Incorporators were appointed the initial trustees with Paige holding the positions of President and Clerk; Henry T. Toepke, a Harvard classmate of Davidson's and QLC Vice President of Sales, the title of Vice President; and Boston business consultant, Arthur Contas, the responsibilities of Treasurer until the first annual meeting of the Board could be held.

Two thousand QLLA memberships were issued to the QLC during the proceedings in White River Junction, along with the understanding that the Board of Trustees had the authorization to discharge more at its discretion. The Corporation agreed, in lieu of assessments or special charges, to assume any net operating deficit incurred in the operation of said amenities until the last of three events transpired:

1. 1,250 active memberships have been issued (originally recognized through the issuance of a certificate)
2. The annual dues of QLLA exceeded $225,000
3. December 31, 1973.

There was never really a first annual meeting of the Board of Trustees. A special meeting was called in its place and was held on October 16, 1971, at the Downer's Mill on Main Street. At the time the meeting was convened, there were 326 active members of the association and 180 were present or represented by proxy. The two major points of business on that first meeting agenda were the election of trustees and the ratification of the proposed changes to the by-laws. The first Board of Trustees elected from the QLLA membership were:

Arthur Blasenberg, Jr.	Elbert G. Moulton
Arthur P. Contas	Hollis S. Paige
L. John Davidson	Donald H. Vance
William T. Dewey	Raymond Van Schoick
Donald A. Gannon	Janet Woodbridge
Norman A. Leader	Clerk - Hollis S. Paige

A month after the Landowners' Association officially came into being, the Quechee Lakes Corporation submitted a document entitled *Declaration of Covenants, Restrictions, Rights and Benefits Pertaining to Quechee Lakes Sub-Division* with the Hartford, Vermont, Town Clerk. This instrument was to be included and incorporated "by reference" into each deed the Corporation conveyed. In other words, anyone purchasing Quechee Lakes property, as well as their heirs and assigns, were required to accept membership in the Quechee Lakes Landowners' Association, and to adhere to a rather long list of constraints the Corporation attached to their property.

Chapter 5

Quechee Lakes Takes Off

In 1969, over 2,000 acres were secured, with options, or right of first refusal, on over 1,000 additional acres. This figure grew to 5,500 by 1971, resulting in QLC's claim to nearly a quarter of the land in the Town of Hartford. With such a vast amount of acreage at their disposal, QLC was able to create amenities—golf courses, ski hills, lakes, and tennis courts—and to build enough homes to support them. The amenities gave it the resort look; the houses added the dimension of community. Together they offered the potential buyer a little piece of Vermont. The completion of Interstates 91 and 89 also provided the development with direct access to major cities.

The dream fast became a reality, and in turn, the largest development of its kind in New England. The concept plan mapped some 2,000 homesites and 500 condominium residences grouped, according to one bit of QLC literature, "within the trees in hamlet arrangements." Open meadow common land and greenbelts insured the buyer a Vermont landscape and a guaranteed view.

By 1971, Kane Financial Corporation and its subsidiary, The Quechee Lakes Corporation, had become part of CNA Financial Corporation. CNA sales in fiscal 1970 were approximately 1.4 billion, with assets estimated at 3.3 billion. Specializing in insurance, real estate, and nuclear power, it was at that time the 51st largest corporation in the United States.

With that kind of financial clout, advertising costs were not a problem. Nor was publicity, for magazine editors from *Yankee* to *National Geographic*, and reporters from the *Rutland Daily Herald* to the *Boston Globe*, wanted the scoop. Slick promotional brochures carried two dozen photographs depicting every aspect of development life, and portrayed a broad range of activities.

Celebrity endorsement was also a part of the promotional plan. The legendary Dave Garroway pitched the development in a

Famed TV personality, Rex Marshall, now WNHV owner and commentator, visits with host Phidias Dantos at gala reopening of Hotel Coolidge.

Phidias Dantos promoted Quechee Lakes by having interested homeowners stay at his hotel and tour the village and homesites.

television piece. In it he says, "I'd like to tell you about a very special place, a place now being created and built, a place where I have some land, called Quechee Lakes—some of the most beautiful land in all New England." He goes on to mention the mill, the lakes and ponds being built, the excitement in taking part in its growth, the action on the championship golf course, the projected ambiance of the clubhouse, the proposed tennis courts and swimming pool.

Needless to say, the ad campaign worked, and prompted others to join those who had already acquired property here the year before. Among those early settlers, those who had committed to Quechee during the first few months of 1970, were Robert and Sybil Cushman, who bought the first renovated property, the Cole Farm; James and Elizabeth Butke, who purchased the first lot, #472; and Jeanne and William Goldbach who became the first condominium owners when they took title to their Birchwood unit.

With so many interested parties, and Purchase and Sales Agreements written, it was now time to put in the mechanism for communal ownership, an association to which all persons purchasing QLC property would be required to join, into place.

By November 1973, the Quechee Lakes sales team had sold in excess of $5.5 million for that year alone. Home site sales in mid-October were $4 million and condominiums $1.5 million. QLC anticipated an active spring for 1974 with 22 home sites awaiting state approval, 63 more units scheduled for spring completion, and 88 Saltbox and 27 Golf Course units planned.

An early advertisement for Quechee Lakes

THE MARK OF ELEGANCE

For those who prefer a very private and special quality home, Quechee Lakes Corporation announces their exclusive line of Elegant Homes.

Select from several architectural designs. For appointments or further information, visit any of our condominium open house models or stop by the Farmhouse Welcome Center on Route 4 on the way to Woodstock. Call 802/295-7527 or write for a full color preview booklet.

Quechee Lakes Corporation

The Quechee Club

For the finest in recreational and dining facilities, come to the Quechee Club. Golf, tennis, swimming and elegant country dining. Contact Peter Labrecque for details... 802-295-9356, ext. 34.

New England's Most Distinctive Prime and Second Home Resort

"Have you ever heard of a new town blended in, around and through a quaint New England village? Unless you know about Quechee Lakes, the answer must certainly be "no," for this is an unprecedented concept in environmental planning and design".
Environment Monthly

"Perhaps what is most impressive is the mix of the community. What has been designed primarily as a second home community with all-year recreational amenities has attracted both young families and retired couples."
Boston Sunday Herald

"...purpose is to keep the open fields open, the magnificent vistas that unfold at every bend in the road, and to tuck the houses themselves into the trees and out of the way."
Christian Science Monitor

"Making environmental excellence a basic condition in the pursuit of corporate gains."
Honor Award Citation · The Environment Monthly Magazine

"Anyone thinking of country living in the world of outdoor activity has got to see Quechee Lakes."
Travel New England

"...one of the ten best new championship courses in the country." **Business Week**

Quechee Lakes, Vermont
(802) 295-7525

Advertising was a key component in the early success of Quechee Lakes.

Chapter 6

Quechee Lakes Changes in Ownership

There are always three entities to be considered in the ongoing history of Quechee Lakes. There is the Quechee Lakes Corporation (QLC), the Quechee Lakes Landowners' Association (QLLA), and the Landowners themselves. In the '70s and '80s, these entities often clashed over different goals and especially budget shortfalls. Many of the executives, owners and presidents changed year by year. In the beginning, the developer held all the votes and hence all of the power. For the first 10 years (1970-1980) Quechee Lakes controlled everything. They built the golf courses, the tennis courts, the club house, and the ski lifts. The annual cost to members was very low as all the amenities were heavily subsidized by the developer.

The second 10 years began in 1980 and as required by their agreement, QLC turned over the ownership to QLLA. The association suddenly had to support itself and assume large expenses. New members were scarce. It was a difficult time, but as the decade went along, QLLA matured financially and in management skills.

The town approved a master plan for the whole development in 1988. There are 5,200 acres in the Quechee Lakes Land Development, one-fifth of all of the land area in the Town of Hartford. Half of the land (2,750 acres) is dedicated as common land and includes 350 acres by the town. The master plan at that time provided for a total of 2,154 residential units, 1,141 single-family houses (approximately 500 had been built by 1989), 749 condominium units (approximately 500 had been built by 1989), and 264 cluster homes.

The history of ownership and management changes begins in 1972. Holly Paige resigned as president of the Quechee Lakes Landowners' Association during the winter of 1972, citing irreconcilable policy differences with the Corporation in general, and it seems, with his best friend, John Davidson, in particular. In turn, Davidson was in the midst of his own difficulties with QLC parent company CNA. The latter had, by this time, acquired a California company called The Larwin Group, and was actively infusing the west coast style of management into their Vermont project.

Effective January 1, 1973, John Davidson resigned as chairman of Quechee Lakes Corporation. "The maturing of Quechee Lakes has made it possible to find reliable and competent personnel. That enables me to hand over with confidence the responsibility of carrying forward the Quechee Concept to its logical conclusion." Owned 87% by CNA Financial, a Chicago headquartered management company, Quechee Lakes is part of the company's real estate division.

Eight months before he resigned from the Corporation, Davidson hired Robert Tuttle to replace Paige as QLLA president. Tuttle, a veteran administrator and club and civic leader, brought with him a host of administrative skills acquired during an airline career that spanned three decades. It was during Tuttle's tenure as president that the Interim Clubhouse was designed and opened, and that the first members information booklet was issued. The latter was intended to supplement information sent to the Landowners in newsletters and in the *Quechee Times*, and was the first comprehensive document of its kind.

Between May of 1972 and September of 1974, while Tuttle was presiding as president, membership had grown to include nearly 700 families, the Larwin Group was directly influencing QLC policy, and QLC established both the Architectural Review Board (ARB) and the Council of Village Enterprise (COVE). Al Moulton was QLC's vice-president at that time, and would succeed Tuttle as president upon Tuttle's resignation in September of 1974. When Moulton took QLLA office in the Fall of 1974, Larwin's Henry Brook was president of QLC. Within six months, Moulton's responsibilities included not only the supervision of the golf course, ski area, lakes, and common lands, but also that of the new clubhouse, the Base Lodge, the red barn, and seven Har-Tru tennis courts. This was no easy task, as the Corporation had begun imposing financial restraints on amenities operations.

The unwelcome rein on spending was the direct result of CNA's own cash flow problems. The parent company solved some of its monetary headaches by selling 57% of its interests to E. M. Lowes, Inc., the national theater and hotel chain. Included in that deal was the Quechee Lakes Corporation. After the takeover, Henry Brook was replaced by Jack Gallaway as QLC President. Gallaway, who had been with Lowes for several years, and had managed some of the conglomerate's more prestigious resorts and hotels, inherited a QLLA operating deficit of $249,000, which the Corporation was committed to pay in monthly installments.

Only one of the three criteria for QLLA independence had been met at this point, that being the December 31, 1973 deadline. The membership in 1975 stood at 1040, and the deficit stated above was greater than the $225,000 dues generated budget allowed in the original documents. Although QLC argued that the recession and gasoline shortages of the period were affecting their sales, amenity use, and QLLA income, they continued with their construction plans and began work on both the Fairway Village and Salt Box condominium projects.

In 1976, Moulton and Gallaway instituted a plan to not only reduce the deficit but which would also set a precedent for the Association. Membership dues were increased.

Gallaway further reduced Corporation costs by deferring QLC payment to QLLA, which resulted in a bad credit line for the Association. Although the Corporation paid an operating deficit of $250,000 for 1975 and agreed to a $200,000 deficit payment for 1976, QLLA auditors figured the loss and Corporation responsibility to be $366,939.

When Moulton left the office of president in the Spring of 1977, four QLLA members were appointed to the Board. Up until 1975, QLC held the majority of seats on the Board of Trustees. The balance of theoretical power was switched at that point with only three Trustees being appointed by the Corporation and the remaining eight being elected by the Landowners. What is perhaps even more important is that the Board, for the first time since its inception, was now installed for a three-year term.

Frederick R. Callowhill replaced Moulton as president, serving in that capacity from May 1977 to May 1978. A retired Air Force Colonel, Callowhill described his term as one "...noted primarily by controversy over money problems as related to QLLA v. QLC." The battle of course was not a new one, but the front lines were changing, and required a new strategy. Callowhill and the "Watchdog" Board were advised by the Corporation that the membership numbers were fast approaching 1,250, and that once they did, QLC would no longer underwrite any deficit incurred by the Association.

Budget discussions absorbed much of the Board meetings, held during the months that followed, but there was little compromise, and no resolution. The Board asked QLC for $600,000 in 1978 to pay the expected 1977 operating loss, deferred maintenance, and working capital. Said monies would constitute a final payment to the Association before QLLA gained its autonomy, which, by rights, was a condition of the original agreement.

Unbeknownst to the Association leadership, however, Gallaway was under strict orders from Lowes not to release or commit any Corporation funds to QLLA.

A special meeting of the membership was called on October 8, 1977 to address this issue, and resulted in the implementation of a two-tier dues structure. The QLLA Base Membership was set at $370, which allowed members the use of all amenities except golf, tennis and skiing. A Full Membership, granting complete use of all the facilities, was set at $490 per year. A one-time assessment of $300 was also passed by the majority. The Corporation's response to these changes was not a favorable one. Faced with marketing the new Mill Run, Quechee Hollow, and Greensway Village condominiums, they argued that such an increase would hinder their sales. In the end, the resulting economy measures QLC had imposed on QLLA, led not only to the resignation of every QLLA Board member, and to Callowhill himself, but also began the long history of lawsuits between the two organizations.

Lawyer John O'Brien succeeded Callowhill as QLLA president in July of 1978.

On September 18, 1978, at roughly the same time the magic numbers of 1,250 Active Members had been reached, QLLA took QLC, CNA, and Lowes to court.

The six counts listed in the complaint petitioned for payment for the cumulative net deficit, asked for clarification on the categories of lots and memberships which were allowed to be counted toward the total of 1250 Active Memberships; requested that QLC file maps and sub-division plats with the Town of Hartford as its failure to do so was resulting in the increased taxes and assessments for the plaintiffs; sought damages relating to QLC's breach of obligation in actively pursuing the sale of QLC properties; asked for the covenants to be declared void; petitioned for a ruling on sewer fees; and finally requested that QLC refrain from altering the greenbelt areas in any way.

This move, it appears, was a necessary one, as QLC was preparing to take complete control of the Association. By December 1978, every position on the Landowners' Board of Trustees, including that of president, was filled by Corporation executives, thus putting John Gallaway in charge of both organizations.

Gallaway maintains that his biggest challenge during this period was "...trying to convince the Landowners that the interests of the Quechee Lakes Corporation and the interests of the Quechee Lakes Landowners' Association were substantially the same." Few among the membership viewed the situation the way he did, including apparently, E.M. Lowes, Inc., the Corporation's parent company. Faced with a lawsuit, which by all accounts was well founded, and with the prospect of incurring further monetary losses, the conglomerate decided that it was time to sell.

In August of 1979, Lowes announced that they had found a "suitable buyer" by the name of David LaRoche. This Providence, Rhode Island resident claimed that he was prepared to assume all of the responsibilities and meet all of the obligations the Corporation carried for the reported sum of 14.9 million dollars. A list of QLLA holdings in November 1979 included:

Lake at Dewey's Mills - 7.07 acres
Birchwood meadow - 31.4 acres
Marshland meadow east of the inn property - 19.8 acres
Village Green - 14.6 acres
Lake Pinneo and Lakeland golf course - 123.6 acres
Highland Golf course - 177.4 acres
Clubhouse, pro shop and Fells Barn - 16 acres
Ski area - 73 acres
Polo field - 37 acres

Lowes sold, and in turn LaRoche conveyed 35% of Corporation stock to fellow Rhode Islanders Charles Gifford and Michael Baker. Gifford, a lawyer, became president of both QLC and QLLA, and Baker, a law student, was appointed treasurer of the Corporation. QLC vice-president, and landscape and design architect, Paul Buff aided the new owners in the transition process. Buff, who had been recruited to QLC by Davidson in 1972 after graduating from Harvard's School of Design, is said to have been instrumental in helping the incoming management gain the Landowners' confidence.

On February 29, 1980, the Quechee Lakes Corporation signed a Memorandum of Agreement, thereby accepting the negotiated settlement of the Class Action Suit. In doing so, the Corporation did, among other things, relinquish its control over the Association by surrendering its QLLA voting rights.

AS A SIGN of future cooperation, the new owner of Quechee Lakes Corp., David F. LaRoche, right, joins hands with Henri V. Dupuis, chairman of the Hartford selectmen, (center) and Jack Galloway, vice president of Quechee Lakes Corp. — Kevin Forrest Photo.

Harvard Law School graduate David M. Marshall became the Landowners' president that year, which was marked not only by the Association's emancipation but also by its adoption of yet another dues structure. Marshall passed the gavel and a $100,000 deficit to T. Olaf Dormsjo after the Annual Meeting in May of 1984. Dmormsjo, who had been recruited as Board clerk by Gallaway in 1979, would become the first QLLA president to experience (due to a shorter fiscal year) a profit in QLLA finances.

LaRoache fired both Gifford and Baker in December of 1981 and bought Gifford's and Baker's shares in QLC, and then elected himself chairman and treasurer of the company he now solely owned. His next course of action was to install Paul Buff as QLC President. Dormsjo and his Board's first priority was to rewrite the QLLA By-Laws. With their governing rules firmly in place, and with the confidence induced by a positive cash flow, the Association began a major capital improvements plan.

When William C. Raitt reflected on his two-year term as QLLA President (1984-1986), he suggested that perhaps his greatest accomplishment was survival, "...to have dodged the barbs and arrows of a number of our dissident land-owners was no small task, but --I survived, the Board survived, and QLLA survived." The Association did prevail. Property was reappraised during Raitt's tenure as president, but perhaps the biggest obstacle the Board faced during this period, and one which posed a major threat to the integrity of the area, revolved around Murphy Farm, the Lakeland area, and The Newton Inn.

A group of private investors known as Uptick had received town approval for a 28-unit condominium project to be built on Murphy Road. The town also gave the developers permission to hook on to the Quechee Lakes sewer system without QLC or QLLA consent and Uptick was actively promoting the timeshare concept. Raitt's efforts, those of his board, and the work undertaken by previous administrations, did in the final analysis insure the survival of the Landowners preferred lifestyle.

Perhaps the most formidable task facing Robert Neilson after taking office as QLLA president in May of 1986 was the resolution of differences between the Corporation and the Association including the QLC sale of Murphy Farm to the Association; the transfer of the maintenance site; the financing provisions in which QLC and QLLA would share the cost of certain added amenities; and measures to strengthen the recommendations of the Architectural Review Board. Neilson, pleased with the results of the negotiations that led to an agreement, was also satisfied with the addition of Murphy Farm to the list of QLLA amenities. "We are not buying Murphy Farm," he said, "just to protect the beauty of the Ottauquechee Valley. We are not buying land and buildings. We are making an investment in what will be a great amenity to be enjoyed by all the Landowners."

Three months after J. Roland Hutcheson rose from veteran board member to QLLA president, the Association purchased Murphy Farm. The closing took place on August 10, 1987. In 1989 QLLA represented $7.5 million in property, and QLC $1 million in land and $3 million in unsold condominiums and lots, and the QLLA owners represented about 140 million dollars.

Leslie Ide became president in May of 1988. The Corporation continued to withhold promised funds and or properties, and the Association met the challenges posed by such a stance through legal recourse. An agreement, which was intended to ease the strain between the Corporation and the Association and to settle differences in an amicable manner, appears to have had the opposite effect.

Paul Buff, President of QLC, Olle Dormsjo, President of QLLA and John Warner, Chairman of the ARB sign agreement on landscaping.

The latest of these was a complaint against the Corporation to recover QLC's cost share of building additional tennis courts. The Landowners, however, gained ground on another point of contention when it was ruled that QLC transfer all greenbelt and common land deeds still in its possession to QLLA.

In June of 1989, LaRoche obtained controlling interest in NECO Enterprises, Inc., which in turn bought QLC and QSC by sale of outstanding stock. In February of 1991 three New England banks petitioned to force David LaRoche to file for Chapter 11 bankruptcy protection. The petition sought a reorganization of Mr. LaRoche's finances to allow him to work out a plan to repay loans. Neither Mr. LaRoche, chairman of NECO Enterprises Inc., nor his lawyer was available to comment. NECO, formerly the Newport Electric Company, is a Rhode Island utility company. In the mid-1980's, Mr. LaRoche's net worth was estimated at more than $30 million.

Chapter 7: Map of Quechee Lakes

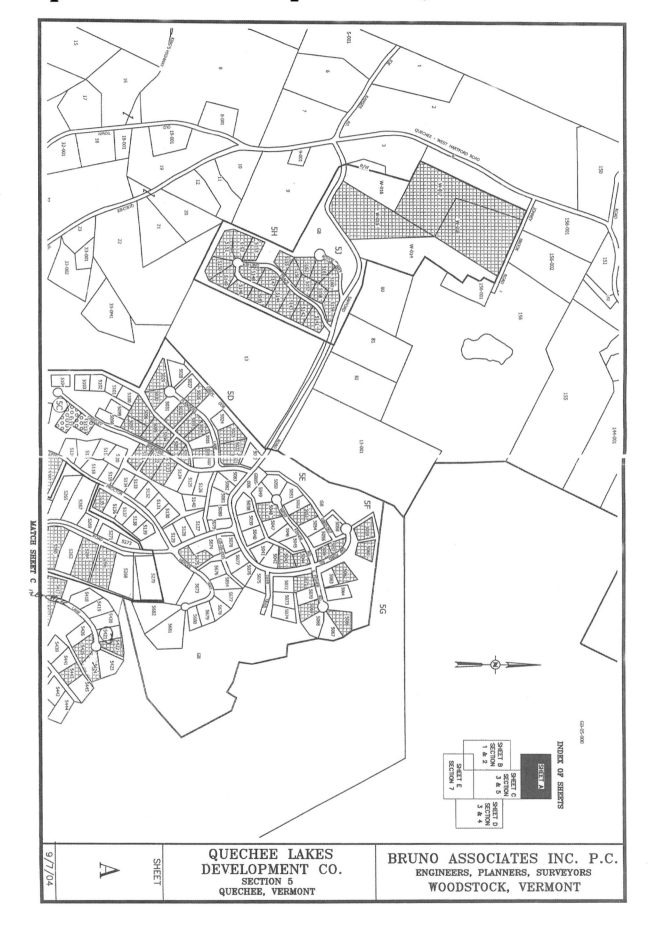

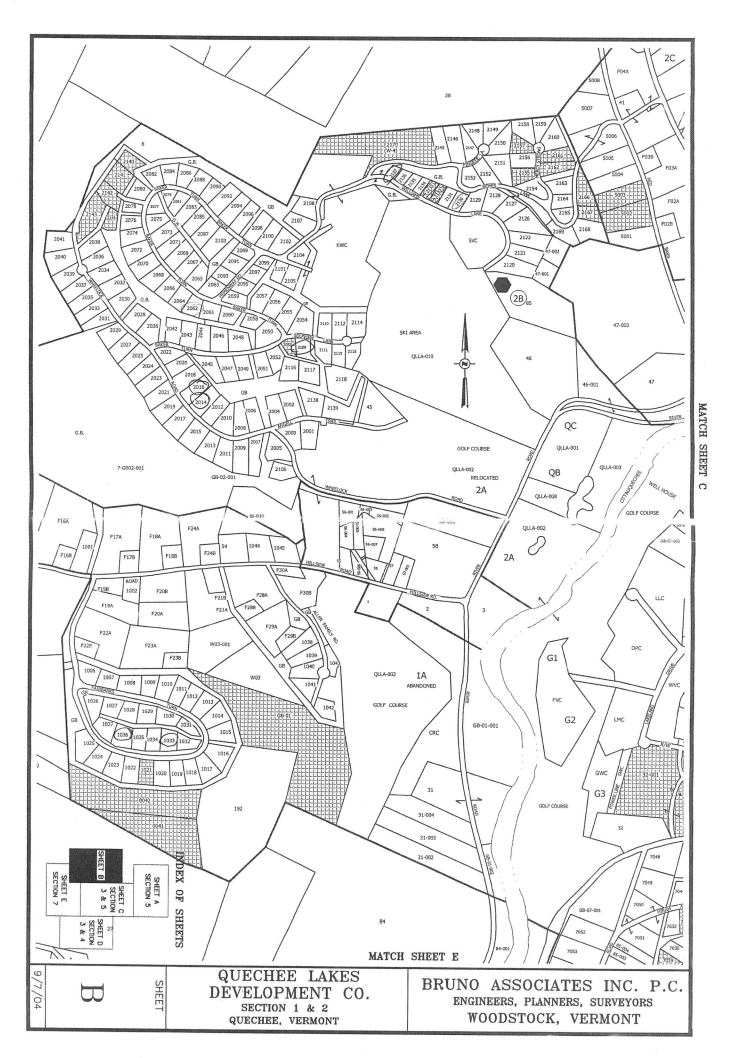

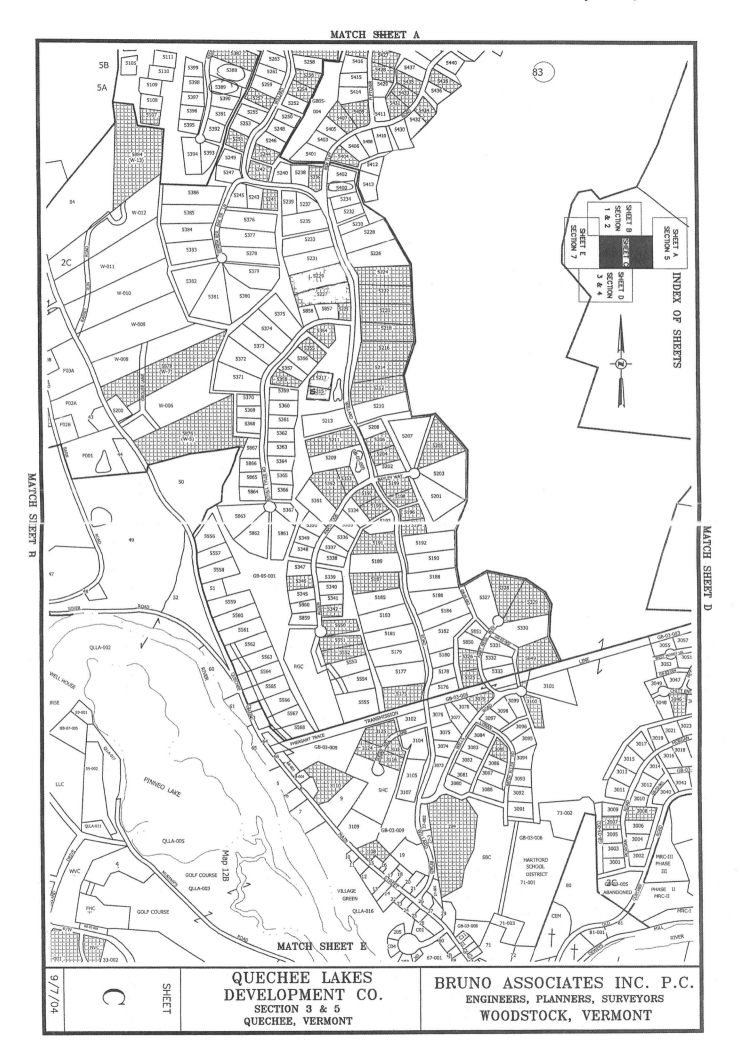

MATCH SHEET A

INDEX OF SHEETS

QUECHEE LAKES DEVELOPMENT CO.
SECTION 3 & 5
QUECHEE, VERMONT

BRUNO ASSOCIATES INC. P.C.
ENGINEERS, PLANNERS, SURVEYORS
WOODSTOCK, VERMONT

9/7/04

SHEET C

MATCH SHEET E

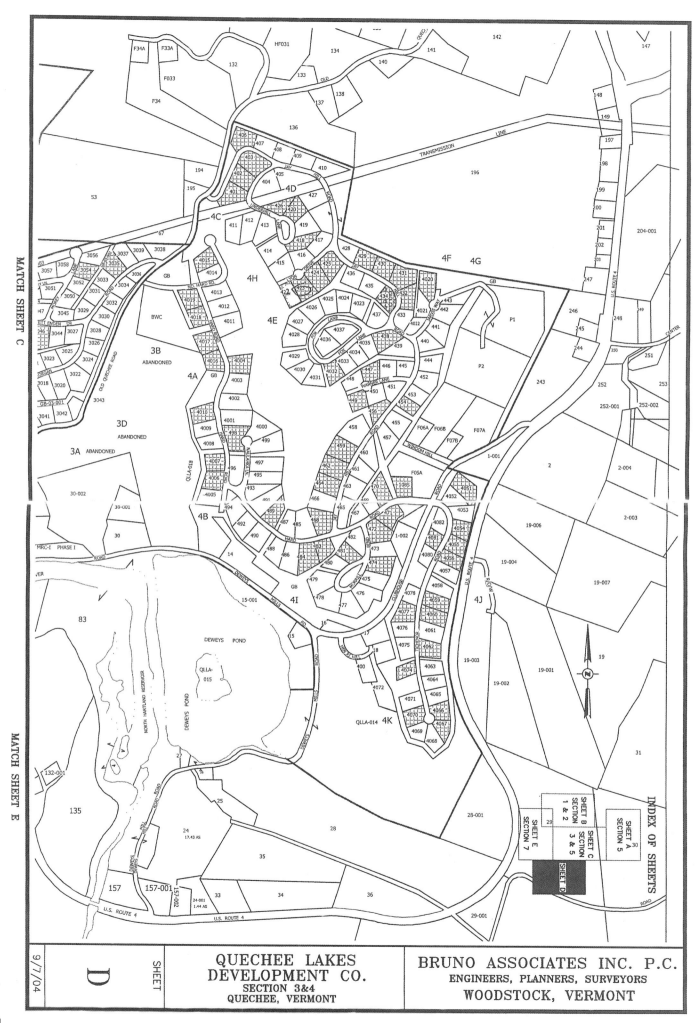

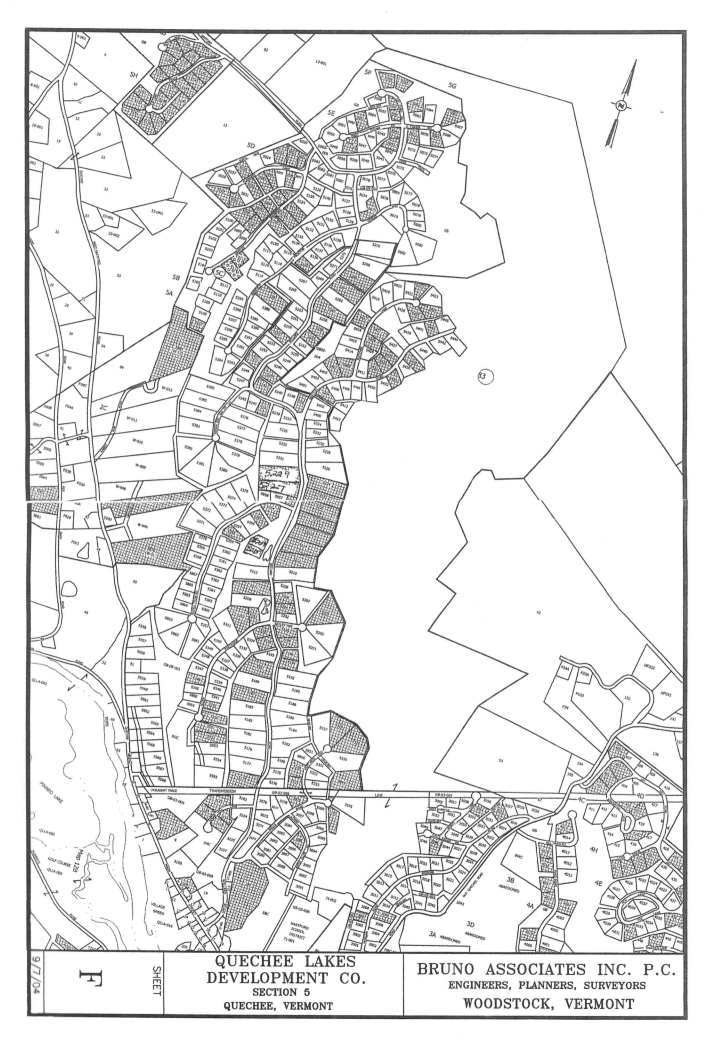

QUECHEE LAKES
DEVELOPMENT CO.
SECTION 5
QUECHEE, VERMONT

BRUNO ASSOCIATES INC. P.C.
ENGINEERS, PLANNERS, SURVEYORS
WOODSTOCK, VERMONT

Chapter 8

The Village of Quechee

An aerial view of Quechee's Main Street

Chapter 8

The Simon Pearce Glass Making Company

The old Downers Mill on Quechee Main Street had changed hands many times before being purchased by two gentlemen from Barre in 1857. J.C. Parker and Co. put the troubled woolen mill back on its feet.

In 1870, the Quechee mill was one of 45 such plants contributing 35% of the 3.5 million dollar revenue the state woolen industry generated that year. Parker's business, and that of A.G. Dewey, were greatly enhanced by the Woodstock Railroad which became totally operational in 1875. J.C. Parker and Co. produced some of the finest white baby flannel, material used to make petticoats, men's shirts and pajamas.

The Quechee mill utilized both water and horsepower to operate 26 looms, 28 card sets, and one elevator. Originally a wooden dam ran a grist mill and grinding floor. A horizontal turbine was installed which ran all of the machinery in the mill through a system of line shafts and large flat bolts. The J. C. Parker Mill, even after the devastating flood of 1869, was producing 30,000 yards of quality flannel a year and employing 50 people.

Times were difficult for Quechee's mills in the 1930s because of numerous factors—the Depression, inexpensive textile mills abroad and the growth of the synthetic industry. The Harris-Emery Mill closed after a workers strike in 1951 and Dewey's Mill at the head of the gorge closed in 1958 when the federal government built a flood control dam downstream. Since it was a potential flood plain, the entire site was condemned by the Army Corps of Engineers and the mill and workers homes were destroyed. Quechee now had a large vacant building in the heart of the village. Windows were broken and streets were littered. Most of the homes were not well maintained and with the rapid decline, people moved away during the 1960s.

Fortunately for Quechee, Simon Pearce and his wife Pia left Ireland in 1980 to settle in Vermont. In the village of Quechee they renovated the old woolen Downers Mill next to a waterfall on the Ottauquechee River and this became the site for the first Simon Pearce glass workshop. They bought the mill and dam which they needed to use the hydro-power to fire their furnace and produce their glassware. Simon Pearce was raised in rural Ireland and was trained as a potter but developed an interest in old glass — glass that was blown and made by hand in the 18th and 19th centuries. He wanted to make simple functional glass that had a similar feeling and character. In Ireland Simon opened his first glass-making workshop in 1971.

The Pearces spent innumerable hours applying for necessary permits, from the Federal Regulatory Commission, from the state of Vermont, the town of Hartford, and the Army Corps of Engineers. When it was all completed the cost of developing the hydroelectric power was initially 1.2 million. He had to excavate through rock in the area beneath the annex building to make room for the turbine. The work involved the installation of the turbine, generator and control equipment in 1983 which made possible the production of electricity. They sold the electric to the local utility and in 1995, they began to use it directly from the generator, generating 2 million kilowatts a year.

The Simon Pearce glass blowing workshop, store and gourmet restaurant is now the highlight of Main Street. Tourists come from all over the country to visit the village of Quechee and the Simon Pearce renovated mill facilities. In the evening the lights of the beautiful glass creations shimmer through the mill windows and light up Quechee Main Street.

Today Simon Pearce is considered to be one of the highest-quality glass making companies in the world.

Above: *The exterior of the Simon Pearce Glass Making Company, store, and restaurant as it stands today*

Right, top: *The windows of Simon Pearce light up Quechee's Main Street at night*

Right, bottom: *A glass artisan at work*

Below: *The shop at Simon Pearce is filled with beautiful handcrafted glass and ceramic pieces*

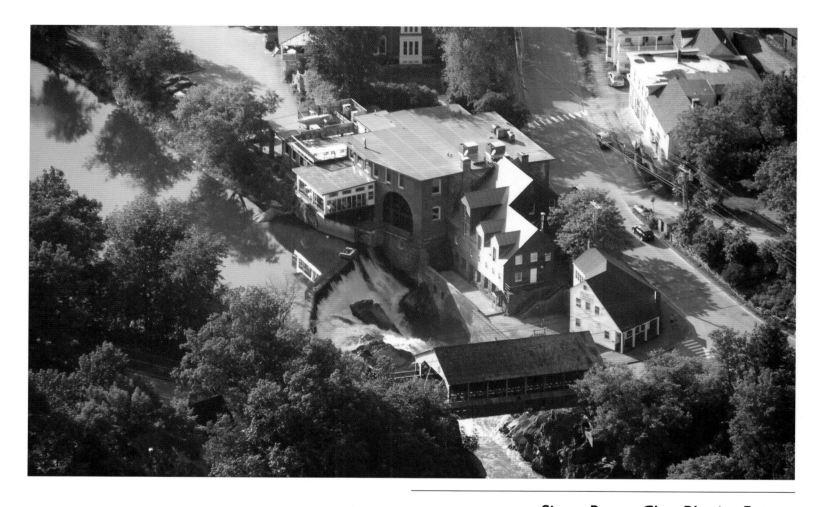

Simon Pearce Glass Blowing Factory

Quechee Gorge Shops and the Antique Mall

New England Specialties Shoppe
The setting is an historic 1870s Dewey Mill-Woodstock railroad freight building with products featuring Vermont and New England made products, gourmet and specialty foods, stoneware, woodenware, linens, candles and more.

Quechee Gorge Village
The Village has many shops featuring furniture and hand-forged iron pieces, Cabot cheese store, Danforth pewter, a country store with handcrafts and gifts, and a glassblowing studio.

This authentic 1946 Worcester diner car was installed and opened in Quechee Gorge Village in 1992. It is now called The Farmers Diner and uses local ingredients from area farmers to make traditional recipes with fresh ingredients. This particular diner is one of seven made by the company in 1946; one is at the Henry Ford Museum and one is at the Smithsonian.

The Library

Citizens of Quechee Village met in 1884 to form the Quechee Library Association. In 1888 the books were housed in Scott Tinkham's store where the post office had been. Then the library moved to the enclosed village bandstand for 14 years. In 1909 a new brick building was built to house the library. In 1995 the building was sold and the former Woodstock National Bank building was bought and renovated in March 1995. The new library opened on the corner of Main Street and Willard, its home today. Many

programs for adults and children are offered to Quechee residents—readings, speakers, used book sales, craft events and afternoon teas to name just a few, under the planning and direction of librarian, Kate Schaal.

Top and right: *the library's home from 1909 to 1995*

Far Right: *the Quechee Library today*

Waterman Place

The Waterman family owned the farmhouse at the top of Waterman Hill in the 1940s. It was originally built in the mid-1800s and was known as the Lewis farm. After remodeling, shops were added, Firestones restaurant opened, and the three-story building became an antiques store.

Quechee Lakes Company

The Quechee Lakes Company is Quechee's largest residential real estate firm. It is owned by an affiliate of Taurus Investment Holdings, LLC of Boston, Massachusetts, an international real estate company. Taurus initially purchased the majority interest in 2005, and purchased the remaining interest in the winter of 2007. The company's principals also own second homes in Quechee.

The Boston office, the headquarters of Taurus Investment Holdings, consists of Taurus New England Investments (TNE), Taurus Capital Markets (TCM), Taurus Capital Funding (TCF), Taurus Corporate Properties (TCP), and Taurus Management Services (TMS). Taurus New England Investments is active in the Greater Boston and New England real estate markets, and has bought and sold nearly 7.5 million square feet of investments over the past decade. TNE focuses on acquiring and developing value-add and opportunistic real estate across all major asset categories, including office, industrial, commercial, retail, and land development.

The Garden Club

The purpose of the Quechee Garden Club is three-fold: To share and encourage the joy of gardening, to sponsor civic projects and beautification, and to further encourage the conservation of natural resources and wildlife.

The first president of the Garden Club was Brad Emerson who established it along with three of her friends in 1988. Members plant and maintain 18 garden spots throughout Quechee including; the Embankment, the Quechee Library and the Village Green, and decorate these same spots for the winter holidays.

Educational programs are held monthly at Murphy Farm. Additional projects include organizing Vermont Clean-Up Day, providing scholarship funds to local college students interested in horticulture, and participating in National Arbor Day. Funds for these projects are raised through the annual plant sale held in May on the Village Green.

Membership is open to everyone. Presently there are 113 members.

Schools of Quechee

The Upper Valley Waldorf School is a private school located in an area which is culturally rich and close to centers of higher learning. Growing steadily since its founding in 1991, the student population is now approaching 150 and offers a full nursery through 8th grade program.

The Ottauquechee School is a public school offering pre-kindergarten through grade 5 and has a student population of about 200. There are a total of 14 spacious classrooms, a gym, cafeteria and kitchen, well-stocked library, dedicated music and art rooms, an outdoor classroom and trail, and playing fields.

Mid Vermont Christian School offers a Christian education for preschoolers through the 12th grade. Students learn in self-contained classrooms, with individual classroom teachers providing instruction. The facilities are located on approximately 10 acres of land. In January 2000, the junior/senior high school was completed and the seventh through twelfth grade moved in as well as the art and music departments, and the computer lab. Presently there are 126 students from preschool through grade 12.

Quechee Gorge

A Swim in the Quechee Gorge under the covered bridge—not for amateurs.

Quechee Gorge known as Vermont's "Little Grand Canyon" is a 3000-feet long, 165-feet deep gorge on the Ottauquechee River. The gorge frames the glacial Devonian Gile Mountain Formation, an ice-contact delta from meltwater streams flowing into Lake Hitchcock. Lake Hitchcock, dammed in the south by a glacial moraine, extended from Connecticut nearly 200 miles north to the Canadian border, with smaller arms extending into present river valleys. When glacial Lake Hitchcock drained, the Ottauquechee River cut quickly through delta sediment, establishing the present course of the Ottauquechee River. It has slowly carved the gorge through bedrock for the past 13,000 years.

The Gorge has become a Quechee tourist attraction providing a spectacular view from the bridge across the river. A path can be hiked to the bottom of the Gorge where often in summer families and teens are swimming and even jumping off the rocks into the deeper spots. Quechee Gorge has become one of Vermont's most popular tourist sites. The Quechee Gorge State Park, VINS, the Gorge, the hiking trails, fishing, canoeing, snowshoeing and cross-country skiing draw over 200,000 visitors a year.

The Ottauquechee River comes down from the Eastern slopes of the Green Mountains and is about 40 miles long and drains more than 220 square miles of terrain; 86% of it forested. It flows mostly unseen in its early miles in fields paralleling Route 4 as it arrows across Killington flat. At Bridgewater Corners where Route 100a intersects Route 4, the river flows under its first bridge, the Bridgewater Corners' bridge.

In November 1927 it started raining torrentially and continued all the next day. The downpour came after heavy October rains had saturated the ground. By the time the rain ended, some places recorded 9 inches. The flood waters claimed 84 lives, including that of the Vermont Lieutenant Governor at the time, S. Hollister Jackson. The flood, often called Vermont's greatest disaster, left 85 dead, 9000 homeless, hundreds of miles of road and railroad tracks washed out, and in all 1285 bridges were washed away. The 1927 flood and another bad one in 1936 provided much of the impetus for the Flood Control Act of 1938 which led to the building of the North Hartland Dam and 15 others.

Above: *Views from the bottom of the Quechee Gorge*

Dewey's Pond

The reclamation of the former millpond as a wildlife refuge was part of Davidson's initial concept. This, the first of two lakes created to give credence to the Corporation's name, centered around "the proposition that the environment there was conducive to such things as foot paths, plantings of flowers characteristic of the area, boating, fishing, and significantly, observation towers within the environment where birds and migratory waterfowl would nest and hatch," according to the May 1971 "Landowners' News Bulletin." The statement goes on to say that "Along with this we expect to have trout and large-mouth bass thriving in this new habitat."

Corporation officials discuss dredging operations at the Lake at Dewey's Mills. When completed, this 50-acre lake will be a wildlife refuge providing nesting areas for several species of waterfowl.

The mill pond became the property of the US Army Corps of Engineers after it was claimed by eminent domain in the early 1960s. The Corps' New England Division leased it to the State of Vermont in 1965 to maintain. The State Department of Water Resources (and later Parks and Recreation) and the Army Corps had a keen interest in preserving and enhancing this active waterfowl site, but neither agency had the funds, so when the Quechee Lakes Corporation approached the state in 1970, and the state in turn petitioned the Army Corps on QLC's behalf, all concerned parties were pleased with the prospects of having the pond reach its full habitat potential.

The Corporation presented its proposal which entailed separating Dewey's Mill Pond from both the Ottauquechee River and the old mill dam using a 2200-foot earth dike with an average width of 50 feet constructed out of the materials produced when dredging the pond; and increasing the water area to its original 50-acre size. The wrinkles were worked out and the reclamation of the pond moved forward, and according to the original plan. Added to this was a proviso that "facilities constructed by the Corporation on government property shall be available for the use of the general public on a free and equal basis." The process of dredging the pond site of accumulated silt and turning 60,000 cubic yards of the same into a dike to prevent a reoccurrence of sediment damage took, all told, three years and a quarter of a million dollars to complete.

The recontoured spring-and-brook-fed pond contains marshy areas for nesting sites, a one-acre island for a waterfowl habitat, and an outlet gate near the dam. Its depths range from 18 inches to 10 feet. Initially, fishing, swimming and the use of powerboats on the pond were prohibited, but fishing and ice fishing as well as swimming, skating, canoeing and kayaking are now permitted and ice fishing in particular is very popular.

The Jedediah Strong House

The Jedediah Strong II House is an excellent example of a house in the high Federal style. Characteristic of a house erected in the Federal period, the house is restrained on the exterior, architectural qualities being limited to subtle articulation and detailing of the wall surface, proportion, scale, and rigid symmetry. In contrast to the exterior, the interior is characteristically less restrained, being highlighted by finely executed architectural details.

The house has historic associations with the Strong family. Solomon, Elijah and Benajah, Jedediah's uncles, farmers and land surveyors from Lebanon, Connecticut, were in 1764 the first permanent settlers in the Town of Hartford, and were in large part responsible for the organization and establishment of the town.

It was probably erected in 1815 or shortly thereafter by Jedediah Strong II, a local entrepreneur, a wealthy farmer, and the owner from 1815 to 1825 of a saw mill and grist mill in Centerville and survives as a symbol of the prosperity which he enjoyed in those positions. The Strong House is now a modern day spa specializing in a wide array of high quality treatments from relaxation to detoxification and injury rehabilitation in a tranquil spa atmosphere.

The Post Office

The Quechee Post Office moved to the Village Green from Main Street in October of 1992. The moving process actually took three years from the time a new site was required because of growth. The 7,600-square-foot facility includes three rental units on the second floor. Simpson Construction of Wilder, Vermont built the structure working from plans by the Grondin/Robinson architects, as well as Steve Crooker's design and the modification by Keith Dewey.

In 1827 Shebel Ross was appointed the first Postmaster of Quechee Village. Charles Tinkham, Scott's brother, served as Postmaster for a period of time from 1868. The Scott Tinkham & Co General Store occupied one side of the clapboard building on Main Street from 1875 with the little post office in the corner of the building distributing letters and newspapers for nearly 100 years from the Tinkham block.

Above: *The Quechee Post Office was located in Scott Tinkham's General Store for 100 years; Charles Tinkham was Postmaster.*

Vermont Institute of Natural Science – VINS

VINS' programs and services engage and instill in people of all backgrounds a desire to care for the wildlife and diverse natural habitats they encounter in their daily lives. VINS has been a leader in environmental education and wildlife conservation and care since 1972 and is known nationally for innovative natural science curricula and education programs for learners of all ages.

VINS offers relevant environmental education programs for adults, families, and school children; partners with leading conservation organizations to promote environmental science field research; and operates New England's premier avian wildlife rehabilitation clinic at the VINS Nature Center. Hands-on public education programs at the VINS Nature Center serve more than 40,000 people throughout New England each year:

> Exhibits – interactive exhibits with frogs, bugs and other creatures
> Live Bird Programs – mechanics of flight, seasonal breeding and migration, avian conservation
> Raptor Enclosures – Northeast's largest collection of birds of prey
> Rehab in Action – feeding baby birds, bandaging wounds, examining new patients
> Pollinator Garden – butterfly and hummingbird pollinator garden
> Nature Trails – 47 acres along the Ottauquechee River

The Parker House

Joseph Chase Parker and his partner Dennison Taft purchased the mill on Main Street in 1857 and Parker built a four-story French second empire-style brick building on the property to house his family. He expanded his business to include numerous other enterprises including farming and lumbering and became very wealthy. He also was a highly-respected Vermont citizen serving as a representative in the general assembly, as a state senator and held several other state positions.

Years after Parker's death Scott Tinkham acquired the property and then left it to his widow Nellie who lost the house to the bank. Kara Childs and her husband bought the mansion and lived there for twenty years until a fire did considerable damage. Quechee Lakes Corporation purchased the property in 1968 for $20,000 and spent $100,000 completely refurbishing it. The mansion was then used as the corporation's headquarters for meetings and to entertain prospective buyers.

Subsequent owners turned the mansion into a restaurant and room rentals were added in 1983. Over the years many talented chefs earned the restaurant a top reputation throughout New England. Today The Parker House continues its tradition of being a fine restaurant and inn.

The Quechee Community Church

The Quechee Vermont Church was started by the Widow Marsh at her home, Marshland Farm, in January 1831. Thus the First Congregational Church was organized.

A building to house it, now Meeting House Restoration, was finished in 1833. The building was donated by Daniel Marsh. In the Gable was an Equilateral Triangle laid in the brick wall. This was a very religious symbol and can be seen from River Street. The building was used as a church until 1869 when the members became disinterested and it was deserted. The church was later sold to school district #3 and still later to the town for a school.

The land for the current church was purchased by W.S. Carter, where a distillery or brewery formerly stood. It was known as the Shubal Russ place. T.W. Silloway, a Boston architect, was employed in 1871 and the church was completed and dedicated on May 23, 1873. On November 12, 1947, the name "Quechee Congregational Society, Incorporated" was adopted.

The Second Quechee Village Meeting-house Society was formed to build a meeting-house in Quechee Village in 1871. T. W. Silloway from Boston designed an Italianate structure with two steeples flanking the gables end and a portico. The turret housed a 1274 lb bell and an organ was installed. Though worship continued for many years, the church was not owned by the Congregationalists until 1948.

In 1961, Rev. Earle Hand, who became the Pastor in 1957, brought up the subject of the Church joining the United Church of Christ. The UCC was formed on July 5, 1957. Rev. Hand read part of its constitution and stated he thought it would be a good plan to unite with the UCC. It was voted on and passed at the annual meeting of 1961.

Over a two-year period murals on the church walls entitled "God's Word in Man" were painted by Kathleen Bruskin, a local artist, in the mid-seventies depicting Bible quotes and themes and using Vermont scenery and local folks in the paintings.

Pastor Jo Shelnutt-Melendy oversees church programs including musical presentations, Children's Sunday, the Christmas Pageant, the coffee project, the choir, and the huge used-item sale during the Hot Air Balloon Festival as well as many others.

The Big Red Barn

The Big Red Barn, now Riverside Farm, in 2010

Main Street in Quechee Village has seen a number of renovations of homes in this abandoned mill town since 1971. The one that sparked the interest is the Big Red Barn. This 1820 post and beam construction is located on the Village Green with views of the Ottauquechee River and the West. There are nine condominiums with 1 to 3 bedrooms - some have lofts and are fully applianced, wall to wall carpet, fireplaces and decks. The lower level of the barn is zoned commercial, and offices are available from 400 to 1,200 sq. ft. This offering will start in January of 1988.

Chapter 9

The Quechee Hot Air Balloon Festival and Craft Fair

For thirty years, every Father's Day weekend, Quechee becomes a mecca for amateur and professional crafters, musicians, and photographers, as the Annual Quechee Balloon Festival & Craft Fair attracts dozens of balloonists and their brilliantly-colored hot-air balloons to our quaint Vermont village.

Left: *The Golden Knights were an exciting highlight of the Balloon Festival in 1978 as they floated to earth with red smoke marking their trail before they opened their colorful parachutes. They returned to the Balloon Festival again in 2010.*

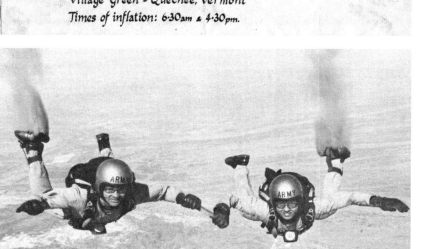

Above: Hot air balloons float over the Quechee Lakes Golf Course
Below: Hot air balloons prepare for lift-off at the annual Quechee Hot Air Balloon Festival

There are as many as sixty outstanding craft artisans from pottery to potpourri. On Friday evenings, the Balloon Glow lights the field as balloons are inflated and rise in the evening sky.

Fortunately for Quechee, in 1979 a group of hot air balloonists were looking for a location to launch their balloons but Woodstock's town fathers voted down the idea of sponsoring a weekend balloon festival. The balloonists had heard about the Quechee village green set on the Ottauquechee River and when they visited the green, they saw it was the perfect location for their hot air balloon festival, a new beautiful home for them in Vermont.

Colorful hot air balloons drift through the sky over Quechee Village Green

Chapter 10

The Quechee Club

The Clubhouse

The Quechee Club offers QLLA members many amenities and choices of activities: golf, skiing, tennis, squash, aquatics, fine and casual dining, the Pro Shop, the Health Club, and recreational planned activities for all ages.

In 2005, a contest was held to name the new four-person chairlift and the winning name was "Quadzilla." The purchase of the new ski lift has been an addition enthusiastically welcomed by QLLA skiers.

The greening of the clubhouse began in the fall of 2008 with an assessment of the green practices and products being used. Based on the results, additional green products were brought in and the club initiated new green practices such as kitchen scraps being donated to local farms, the recycling of styrofoam cups, and recycling stations throughout the club. Due to these changes there has been an overall reduction in waste at the club. In October of 2009, an Anything-With-a-Plug disposal program began for QLLA members and the Quechee community as well, in order to keep items such as refrigerators, televisions, and computers out of local landfills.

History

***Above:** The Quechee Club in the 1970s;*
***Right:** A Landowners' meeting overflows*

The Quechee Lakes Landowners' Association has had three club sites over the last twenty-five years, all of which have occupied some portion of the 425-acre Quechee Fells Farm once owned by Harold Eastman. QLLA's first gathering space was in what is now known as the Base Lodge, and was once the home of Eastman's hired hands. The club activities, the Pro Shop, and what was then coined the "19th Hole" were all housed in this building.

In 1972, plans were in the works to move the Clubhouse to the big red barn across the road. The newly formed "House Committee" was responsible for converting former hay storage, stable and milking operations areas into a cozy, comfortable and stylish gathering place. The results of the committee's efforts was known as "The Interim Clubhouse," and opened on a limited basis on December 31, 1973. Over one hundred and twenty-five landowners and their guests rang in the New Year with a gala celebration, which included Scottish ballads and dance tunes. The Interim Clubhouse officially opened on February 15, 1973, offering tablecloth dining, with a full menu and legal beverages on the first floor, and a bar serviced lounge on the second level. The Interim Clubhouse closed on March 17, 1974, and during the months that followed the space was refurbished to meet the needs of QLLA's younger members.

On March 2, 1973 the foundation of the main clubhouse was christened. Construction of the $1,000,000, 33,000 square-foot complex, which would stand on the site of the old farm junkyard, began in April. Designed by the same company who drew up the Kingswood and Snow Village condominium complexes, Environmental Systems, Inc., of Brookline, MA, it was built by Trumbell Nelson of Hanover, NH. The original drawings called for a clubroom, locker rooms, a whirlpool, offices,

a health club, sauna, and a 192-seat dining room which opened on to a 5,000 square-foot deck.

It took a full four days to officially open the new Clubhouse. Festivities began with a Governor's Preview on May 16th, listing then Vermont Governor Thomas P. Salmon, and former Governors Dean Davis and Phillip Hoff as the guests of honor. Dignitaries from CNA and the Town of Hartford were also invited to this black tie affair. The landowners had their first glimpse of the new facility during a dinner dance held for them the following evening.

On Saturday, May 18, 1974, Walter French, Quechee's oldest resident, hoisted the American flag in front of the new Clubhouse. L. John Davidson then cut the ceremonial ribbon accompanied by a fifteen-piece brass band. That evening, after the business of the fourth annual QLLA Landowners' meeting was concluded, an opening night dinner dance was held. On October 11, 1974, the QLLA Board of Trustees accepted responsibility for managing the Club's operation and activities schedule although QLC continued to meet its financial obligations.

The Thanksgiving dinner of 1975 is one to be remembered with some pain and much humor. The Club had a large number of reservations for the traditional feast, which necessitated cooking more birds than the kitchen could handle. The turkeys were farmed out to be baked in the ovens of QLLA members. Apparently everyone was quite agreeable and received the turkeys delivered on aluminum-covered trays. Many of the volunteers put the aluminum covered trays in the oven and since they were made of plastic, they not only melted in the ovens but left a strong smell which permeated their homes.

Next, the Club expanded its dining services to include a less formal atmosphere by offering grille service on the deck. Fast food service was still available at the 19th Hole. The landowners voted to open the Club to the public during their 1979 Annual Meeting, and gave the Board the go ahead to lease the food concessions for both the dining room and the 19th Hole. A year later the Club returned to its private status, save for what were deemed very special occasions. This decision was made at a Board meeting held

shortly after the Club had undergone major refurbishing. Carpets were replaced; the lobby was filled with new furniture; the entire building received a fresh coat of paint; and the deck was covered with a new green rug. In 1982, the longest canopy in Vermont, produced by Metzger Brothers of Rutland, topped the Clubhouse deck. It stood for only a year, however, because the platform it covered had to be completely rebuilt in 1983. The entire building underwent major refurbishing the following year, which included the expansion of the main lounge and the addition of new glass double doors opening off of it. By incorporating this feature, food and beverage was able to service two sizable functions simultaneously.

One of the most engrossing and time consuming Clubhouse renovations took place during the latter half of 1990 and the early

months of 1991. Referred to as the "front wall project," this massive undertaking involved the stabilization of the front wall. The process began with a plan devised by Construction Drillers, Inc.

(CDI) of North Adams, MA, and required the placement of approximately 90 thirty-foot anchor rods. These rebars were installed from the interior of the structure so that there would be little disturbance to either the exterior facade or the members use of limited facilities. The thirty-foot metal rods were passed through the walls and anchored in the ground, then torqued to prevent further movement. The stabilization process went well and the Clubhouse was re-opened on May 17, 1991.

Plans were drawn during the fall of 1993 to convert the lounge area of the Clubhouse into a Grille Room. The renovations were undertaken, according to General Manager, Paul Zeno, because "Many of the members, especially those driving or flying in for the weekend, have expressed their wish to have a casual restaurant at the Clubhouse." The Lycett Company of Quechee was responsible for the constructional transformation of the entry-level floor space, and Regina Caruso, of Lebanon, New Hampshire's Design Plus for pulling together the interior furnishings. The Grille Room became QLLA's fourth eatery when it opened on December 8, 1993.

The most recent Clubhouse renovation project was approved by the membership in August 2004. The Board of Trustees gave the House Committee the task of selecting an interior designer. In April 2005, after much legwork by the committee, Richard C. Eustice of Atlantic House Limited, Marblehead, Massachusetts was selected for the job.

Actual construction on the Clubhouse was begun in September 2005. Prior to this, twice monthly meetings were held to select all of the furnishings, lighting, interior paint colors, wall coverings, flooring and decorative items for all of the interior spaces and outdoor decks. Transformation started to take shape in early spring 2006 with the new exterior paint colors and the installation of fireplace in the lobby. When work was progressing the contractor discovered problems with drainage, leaking, electrical and structural elements that were unexpected.

The Quechee Clubhouse will be undergoing necessary restoration of the front wall this winter which will restrict its use for several months above and below it, the skiing will be fine as ever.

The ladies at bridge on Wednesdays - A very popular indoor sport.

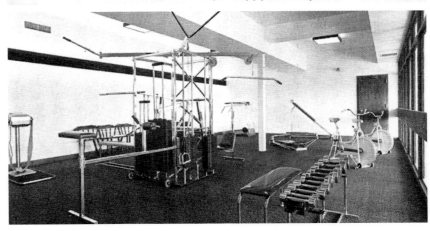

The original exercise facilities at the Club

Major furnishings were delivered on May 26, 2006. Richard Eustice and his staff worked 12-hour days for over a week to meet the June 3rd deadline. It is hard to believe that a project of this magnitude was accomplished in nine months, on schedule, and on budget. During the renovation, the administrative offices were moved to the tennis center, the Health Club was moved to the basement of the Base Lodge, and dining was in Murphy Farm.

Currently in 2009 and 2010

The Club has expanded its dining options with TQC Food-to-Go and Grab-and-Go food stations in the Base Lodge as well as breakfast and lunch. QLLA members continue to have fine dinners in the Grille Room and summer lunch and dinner on the club-house deck. Specially priced meals on Thursdays were offered in the winter and were very successful at attracting more diners. Facilities were generously donated for CHaD and Haven events.

Photos of the renovation of the Quechee Club, September 2005 - June 2006

Above: The Quechee Club today

Below, clockwise from top left: Clubhouse lobby; Clubhouse Grille Room; CHaD Gala 2010 held on the Quechee Club's covered deck; Clubhouse entrance

Golf

The courses at Quechee have been, since the day they were built, the most scenic, well-maintained, and challenging in the state.

In 1969, Richard Johnson contacted two gentlemen from an Amherst, MA business called Fiddler's Green, to inspect the new development and to help choose a site for a golf course. Their names were Geoffrey Cornish and William G. Robinson, and they were rapidly becoming two of the foremost golf course architects in North America.

Young golfers getting started the right way

Cornish was influenced by, and studied with, world-renowned designer, Stanley Thompson, and later taught subjects related to golf course design, construction and maintenance at the University of Massachusetts, Amherst. Robinson, on the other hand, held a degree in Landscape Architecture. The variety and difficulty of both Highland and Lakeland give testimony to their combined creativity and skill.

Cornish and Robinson toured the land owned by the Corporation's Massachusetts based landscape consultants, Sasaki, Dawson and Demay, Inc. A site was chosen near the river, and construction began the following year. The latter included importing special sand for the new traps, and seeding with the best grass blends money could buy. In May of 1971, the first nine holes, built by International Golf Construction, were opened for play. The same company completed the back nine in 1972. The original course included what are now known as Highland 1 & 2, and 9-18, and Lakeland 1-4, and 17 & 18. It also claimed one of only three underground watering systems in the state.

After an exciting season of full round play, Mother Nature wreaked havoc. On June 30 and July 1, 1973 the waters of the Ottauquechee River rose to unfathomable heights, leaving in its wake a course littered with salt and debris, and a bridge connecting the links in ruin. The swift and effective cleanup efforts amazed Cornish. In fact, hundreds took part in this massive reclamation project, including those who replaced the washed out bridge. Boston engineering firm, Theodore Weaver Associates, was engaged to design a permanent span that would withstand "the pressures of high-water." The Pinello Construction Co., of Burlington, VT began work on the new bridge in mid-July, and completed the $40,000 structure on October 1, 1973.

New plans were drawn up for the course in 1974, due to the impending construction of Lake Pinneo. The end result was the creation of two courses, the second designed by Cornish and built by The Moulton Construction Company of Lebanon, New Hampshire. The million dollar project was completed in July of 1976, making the 36- hole layout, according to a local newspaper report "...one of the largest private golf complexes in New England...devoting some 250 acres...to the sport."

An invitational tournament christened the new course, called Lakeland, on July 22. 1976. Government officials, business leaders and a host of other dignitaries gathered in Quechee for this event. A few days after the pomp and

An eager golfing fan leads the pack as an eager audience followed Bob Lendzion to the third place finish in the New England Open on the final day played on the Highland course.

circumstances subsided, a system of rotating play was instituted to insure members their tee time. The other course, Highland, was made available to Junior Club Members, guests and tenants.

In 1977, a new bridge was built over the Ottauquechee, replacing the 1973 structure. This one, designed by Charles Bacon, of Woodstock, VT., and built by Miller Construction Company of Windsor, VT, stood six feet higher than its predecessor, and two feet wider. It was engineered for greater carrying capacity and maintenance equipment accessibility. Unlike the other, the new bridge was assembled in four sections, each weighing about 10 ton, and devised so that they could be removed in the event of high-water.

The new Lakeland course was, by Landowners' vote, opened to the public during the 1977 season in the Association's hopes of generating much needed income. Access to Highland, however, was strictly limited to QLLA members and their guests.

The Highland golf course was the site of the New England Amateur Golf Tournament in July 1977 with the best amateur golf players in the six-state region vying to be 1977 New England amateur champion.

The year 1980 brought a lot of publicity to the links. Quechee was featured on the cover of, and had a four-page spread in

The New England Professional Golfers Association Magazine; ice cakes covered the course; and the Club held its first New England Open Golf Tournament, followed by a Pro-Am.

The Corporation was responsible for bringing the tournament here, underwriting its guarantees supplemented by a limited number of cosponsors. People were not only excited by the prospects of the upcoming event, but also by the buzz that President Gerald Ford may be in attendance. Unfortunately, the demands of the world leader's schedule prevented him form doing so, but the charity fund-raiser for local hospitals was a huge success nonetheless. This event was also the impetus behind the creation of QLLA Charities, Inc.

Both courses were deemed private in 1983, but the Board decided that sponsored groups would be allowed the use of Lakeland as required. The regularly-inspected links were re-measured with laser beam equipment that year, and re-rated by the USGA. This was also the year of the first Golf-Tennis Biathlon, the reinstitution of the Quechee Invitational, and the Vermont State Finals American Cancer Society Golf Tournament.

The 18 holes of Lakeland had to be re-built in 1984 to accommodate new condominium construction, and the bridge over the Ottauquechee required and underwent renovation. The season opened with Highland ranking in the top 1% of all United States

golf courses, according to the American Society of Golf Course Architects.

Government officials, business leaders and others gathered to celebrate the opening of the second 18-hole golf course at Quechee Lakes. The one million dollar Lakeland course designed by Geoffrey Cornish and William Robinson combined with the earlier Highland course devotes some 250 acres to golf, making the 36-hole layout one of the largest private golf complexes in New England.

Like other amenities in Quechee Lakes the new golf course was turned over debt-free to the Quechee Lakes Landowners' Association. The other facilities have been deeded to the landowners already. Cornish and Robinson, golf course architects of Amherst, Massachusetts, who also designed the Highland Course, were present at the opening event along with John Galloway, Executive Vice President of Quechee Lakes Corp and Elbert Moulton, President of the Quechee Lakes Landowners' Association.

A ribbon cutting was held in 1977 for the new bridge spanning the Ottauquechee River connecting the Highland and Lakeland golf courses, 180 feet long, elevated two feet wider and six feet higher than the original bridge.

Top: *Lake Pinneo and the Lakeland Golf Course*
Above: *The beautiful colors of autumn foliage grace the Highland Course; The golf bridge now solidly in place over the Ottauquechee River, having been rebuilt many times over the years due to ice blocks and flooding.*

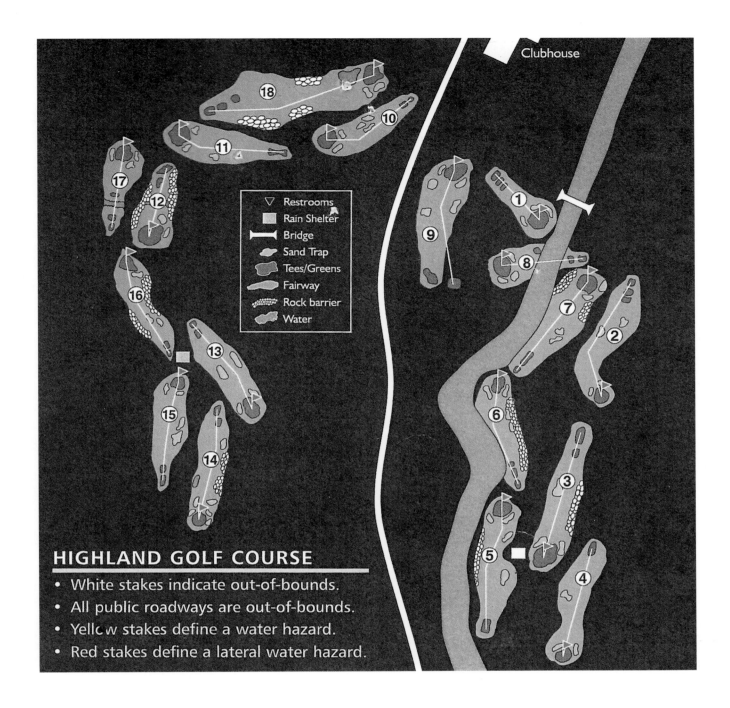

Clubhouse

Legend

▽ Restrooms
▢ Rain Shelter
⊢⊣ Bridge
Sand Trap
Tees/Greens
Fairway
Rock barrier
Water

HIGHLAND GOLF COURSE

- White stakes indicate out-of-bounds.
- All public roadways are out-of-bounds.
- Yellow stakes define a water hazard.
- Red stakes define a lateral water hazard.

The Highland Golf Course

The Highland Course has the distinction of being named #1 in the State of Vermont by *Golf Digest*. Playing 6570 from the back tees, the Highland Course is more of the links-style design that incorporates trees, bunkers, and water features.

Encircled in many areas by stands of trees, and defined by dramatic elevation changes from tee box to green on a variety of holes, this course encourages strategic play and accurate shooting. A number of side hill lies and panoramic views add to the challenge of staying focused and getting that low score.

Highland Golf Course Details:

Course Architect:
Geoffrey Cornish

Gold Tee Yardage: 6,780 yards
Blue Tee Yardage: 6,448
White Tee Yardage: 6,167
Red Tee Yardage: 5,395
Par: 72

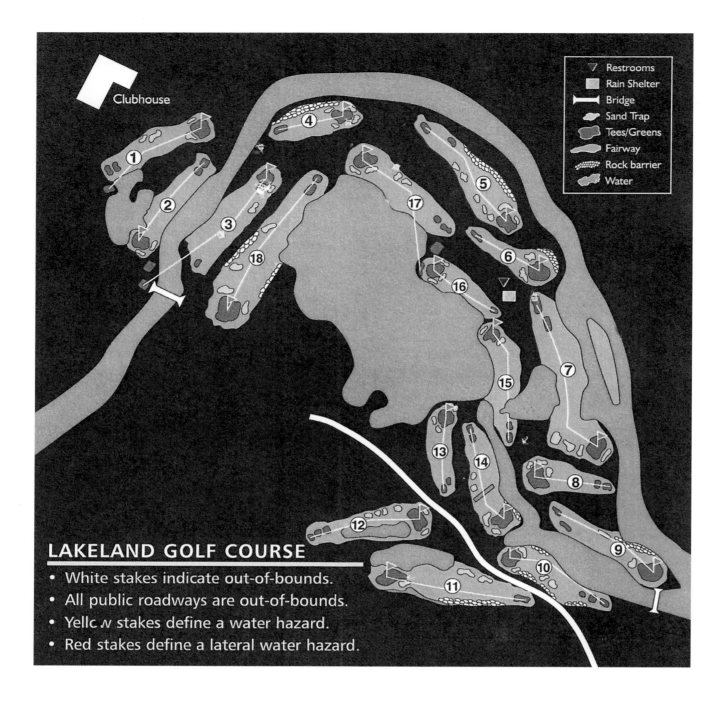

LAKELAND GOLF COURSE

- White stakes indicate out-of-bounds.
- All public roadways are out-of-bounds.
- Yellow stakes define a water hazard.
- Red stakes define a lateral water hazard.

Legend:
- ▽ Restrooms
- ▢ Rain Shelter
- Bridge
- Sand Trap
- Tees/Greens
- Fairway
- Rock barrier
- Water

Clubhouse

The Lakeland Golf Course

The Lakeland Course measures just over 6765 yards from
the back tees and presents more of a links-style design that
incorporates trees, bunkers, and water features, a combination
of gently rolling and elevated tree-lined fairways, along with
rock walls and bunkers. A long stretch of the Ottauquechee
River runs adjacent to the course, making ball placement and
skillful course management key to a successful round. Its rolling
and generally wide fairways often allow the ball to gain extra
distance off the tees.

Lakeland Golf Course Details:

Course Architect:
Geoffrey Cornish

Gold Tee Yardage: 6,583 yards
Blue Tee Yardage: 6,201
White Tee Yardage: 5,921
Red Tee Yardage: 5,319
Par: 72

Quechee Club Champions

	MEN	WOMEN
1972	Bill Goldbach	
1973	Joe Hayes III	Jean Talmage
1974	Bill Purcell	Ruth Katz
1975	Bill Purcell	Ruth Katz
1976	Bill Purcell	Jean Talmage
1977	George Grimm	Jerry Russell
1978	Bill Purcell	Jean Talmage
1979	Jack Hatcher, Jr	Jean Talmage
1980	Ed Holland	Ruth Katz
1981	Bill Pursell	Nancy Guerin
1982	Bill Pursell	Nancy Guerin
1983	Donald Brief	Nancy Guerin
1984	Chester Davis	Nancy Guerin
1985	Terry Deleo	Nancy Guerin
1986	Kerry McNamara	Nancy Guerin
1987	Terry Deleo	Nancy Guerin
1988	Terry Deleo	Mary Lou Ketchum
1989	Kerry McNamara	Sue Chmieleski
1990	Rod Beebe	Chris Wilder
1991	Rod Beebe	Nancy Guerin
1992	Terry Deleo	Sue Chmieleski
1993	Terry Deleo	Rene Leoni
1994	Terry Deleo	Nancy Guerin
1995	Mike Fox	Chris Wilder
1996	Rod Beebe	Rita Kennedy
1997	Jim Keighley	Kathy Hansen
1998	Ned Waters	Sue Norton
1999	Dave Murray	Carol Dawson
2000	Jim Keighley	Lisa Lacasse
2001	Jim Keighley	Kathy Hansen
2002	Ned Waters	Rita Kennedy
2003	Jim Keighley	Michelle Marcus
2004	Ned Waters	Carol Dawson
2005	Mike Nesseralla	Pat Decaire
2006	Ned Waters	Lisa Lacasse
2007	Jim Keighley	Pat Decaire
2008	Jim Keighley	Shelley Yusko
2009	Bill Dwyer, Jr.	Sarah Clunan
2010	William Dwyer	Pat Decaire

Above: *The view of the Ottauquechee River from the golf bridge as it flows onward to Woodstock*

Chapter 10

Skiing

Quechee Lakes, in its 38th year of operation, has its own downhill ski area, 13 trails and 100 acres of skiing terrain, ideal for beginners, children and intermediate skiers. There are 10 trails, a T-bar, junior lift, snowmaking and a new chair lift, (named in a contest "Quadzilla"), 2700 feet in length. The elevation at the top is 1250 feet and the vertical drop is 650 feet. Alpine, cross-country and snowboard instruction are available. There are also 15 kilometers of marked cross-country trails on the golf courses and 15 on hilly terrain in heavily wooded section 5.

The Quechee Ski Hill opened in the winter of 1970-71 carrying enthusiastic members 2700 feet to the top of one of three intermediate trails. The less adventurous landowners' climbed the gentler slopes on a rope tow. "Dewey's Drop," designed for the advanced Alpine skiers, was opened the following year.

Ski patrol fixes up donated cabin.

The facility became so popular that, in 1974, an extra day of skiing was added, giving members access to the hill from Friday through Monday, and complete weeks during three major school vacations. A fully-accredited 14-member Ski Patrol was formed that winter to safeguard the trails and assist skiers in need.

By 1978 a Tucker 1642, a vehicle boasting an 8-way blade capable of cutting moguls and moving snow, and a compactor bar able to compress the white stuff were added. The Tucker, Spryte, rollers, and powder makers provided the Ski Hill crew with the tools to create favorable conditions, assuming of course, Mother Nature supplied the basic ingredients required for success.

The famous New England retail store, Carroll Reed, took seasonal possession of the Golf Shop in the Base Lodge in 1978, offering cross-country and alpine equipment, as well as other items catering to the skier's needs. Besides managing the shop, Bill Wheeler offered ski lessons in downhill, free-style and racing techniques using the Short Ski American Teaching Method. His presence qualified Quechee for membership in The Professional Ski Instructors of America Ski School Association.

Perhaps the most beneficial addition to the ski hill came in 1983, when heated discussions began concerning the acquisition of snow making equipment. The preliminary findings of a feasibility study conducted by engineering consultants Alford International were presented to the Board by the Ski Committee in January of that year, and indicated that such a purchase, with its related expenditures, would run in the neighborhood of $300,000. The Trustees conferred on the issue for two months before resolving to proceed with the project

The membership voted to approve the project and on June 22, 1983 a hearing was held with the District Environmental Commission at the Club to discuss an application for a permit to construct the underground snowmaking line and required pump house. Mounds of documents had to be presented to the Commission at the Act 250 hearing. A provisional permit was obtained from the Stream Alteration

Young skiers hitch a ride to the tows.

A beautiful pair of grays pull a wagonfull of skiers from base lodge to hill and back if too tired to walk.

One of six fan jets which will make the snow this winter is demonstrated on the practice tee.

Vermont Act "250" Permit for Snowmaking Arduous But Effective Procedure

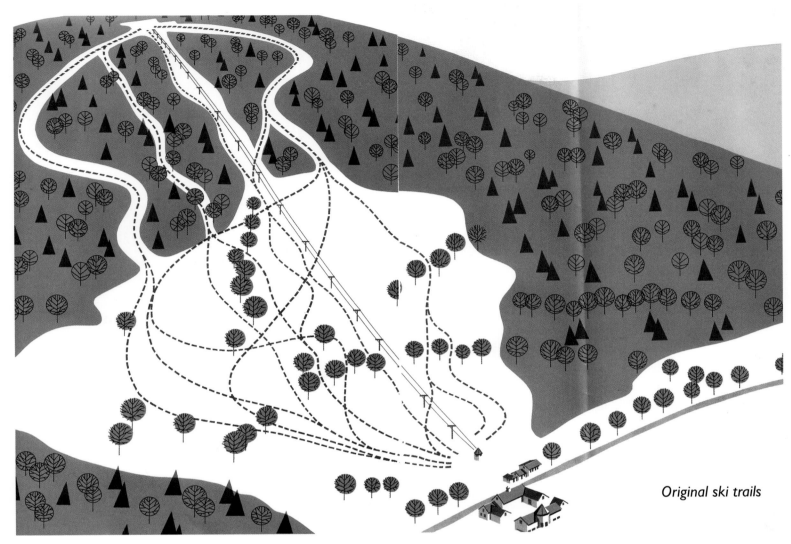

Original ski trails

Agency approving changes in water flow, as the water to be drawn for snow production would be obtained from Lake Pinneo using a main buried ten feet below the surface of the ground. All the paper gathering paid off in the end, for in December of 1983 the Quechee Ski Hill had the ability to produce its own snow.

The Quechee Ski Hill being a south facing hill, and the only south facing ski hill in Vermont, with the addition of snow making equipment, has been able to provide the enjoyment of sunny skiing even when the weather does not cooperate with snowfall.

Torchlight parades became very popular on the Quechee slopes during the mid-1980s. A particularly ornate run took place in 1986 during the George Washington birthday weekend, when over 50 Alpine skiers equipped with flares descended the slopes. They skied towards a bonfire, and the word Quechee spelled out in burning light positioned at the foot of the hill. The slopes were also graced during that season by the presence of the 1985 US Combined Freestyle Champion, Chuck Martin, who demonstrated his abilities to an awed and appreciative crowd.

The membership went before the Environmental Commission again in 1986 to make some minor changes to the existing runs. Alterations to Stage Coach, Dewey's Drop, and the Quechee Express were aimed at facilitating traffic flow, improving skier safety, and enhancing the overall aesthetics of the hill. The proposed changes would also impact the area surrounding the 1500-foot T-Bar, which had been installed along the western edge of the Plateau in 1975. Mel's Run was cut in 1987 giving more variety to the intermediate-expert skiers. This addition brought the trail total to five, which is where it currently remains.

Saturday ski races

The ski school offered lessons in the use of this new Alpine phenomena called Snowboarding in 1988, and an area was provided for practice until individuals

The beginning of the new cross country trail, taken just before the big January snow. It is beautiful for walking and will be even better for skiing.

The x-country ski trail has been marked and groomed for the intermediate and expert in Section Five.

obtained the necessary certification for using the equipment on the slopes. Snowboarders had the added advantage of applying their new skills over a longer period, because the hill was open on a daily basis throughout the month of February. This extended period of access to the slopes was also beneficial to the newly formed ski team.

By 1991, the arsenal of snowmaking guns had increased to ten, and the purchase of a new Pisten Buddy 240 Groomer was in the works. The Spryte was retired once the new machinery was acquired, leaving the '74 Tucker, the '83 Pisten Bulley 170, and the new 240 to groom the highways and byways of the hill. Although the instillation of a fixed Bullwheel, a raised loading station, and a new ticket booth may be of interest to some, the big news for QLLA skiers and the general public invited to "SKI QUECHEE" came in 1992. That is when Quechee conditions gained as much notoriety as its internationally known neighbors, by having its conditions listed in the Associated Press Ski Report. Yet regardless of its newfound status, Quechee remains a family ski area, providing landowners with quality conditions, not only on the slopes but on its cross-country trails as well.

Cross-country skiing has existed in the development from the beginning, with trails cutting through hundreds of acres of woods and meadows. It took nearly a decade, however, for the Nordic facilities to really get on track. The climate surrounding this sport truly began to change with the first Quechee Classic, a 6.2K race held in both 1981 and 1982. The facilities available for cross-country enthusiasts expanded considerably in 1983 when the Corporation transferred ownership of 1,000 acres of land in Section 5 to the Association. In addition to tracking the golf course, 10 miles of trail were cleared in Section 5, which were initially intended to double as biking and riding paths in the warmer months.

US Biathlon Olympic skier, Don Neilson, said of the site, "...nowhere in the state...is there such a piece of land with the features of ready access, gentle and eminently varied terrain, protection from the wind at all parts, good drainage and freedom of road crossing." 15K of trail has been tracked here after every storm since 1991. The most popularly used portion of the total 30K track available, however, lies on the golf course and around Lake Pinneo.

The Quechee Ski Team

The Quechee Alpine Ski Club (the "Quechee Ski Team") was established back in 1987 by Quechee ski hill's current Ski Patrol Director, Dave Courtney. In its first year of existence there were approximately 25 young athletes in the race program all coached by enthusiastic parents. More than 20 years later the team is now an established member of the Vermont Alpine Racing Association ("VARA") with a program that has grown to a point that each winter more than 100 children from 7-18 years of age participate in a training and race schedule that, depending on age and ability, can be seen racing slalom, giant slalom or super-G at mountains throughout mid-Vermont, including Ascutney, Killington, Middlebury, Okemo, Pico, Suicide Six and, of course, Quechee!

The team's annual fun race is the Quechee Cup, where fancy dress costumes are as much a part of the race as the time it takes to get from the start gate to the finish line. While parents are still an integral part of the program, their role has increasingly shifted from coaching to a focus on the team's Board of Directors and in volunteering for the many positions that need to be filled on those days that Quechee hosts VARA races—including gate judge, starter, finish referee, timing, course maintenance, and, most important, vocal supporter.

The crucial role of coaching is now managed by a dedicated program director and a team of more than 10 qualified and paid coaches, some of whom have passed on their experiences as US Olympic team members and gold medal winners on the international world cup ski circuit. The coaches' role is to help the young athletes develop their ski racing skills in a safe and friendly environment but, as with many of the activities that one can pursue in Quechee, with an emphasis on fun.

Above (left): Skiers hit the slopes on a perfect winter day in Quechee

Above (right): Fireworks light up the ski slopes

Left: The Base Lodge is the place for après ski snacks and light meals, and for the young people's recreation area.

Tennis

The Quechee Club now has 11 tennis courts, eight of which are Har-Tru. Several condominium villages have their own courts as well.

The earliest three courts were constructed in 1971 on the south side of Main Street to the west of the clubhouse. They were red clay and fenced in chicken wire. A second set was built in 1972 of asphalt.

It's never too early to develop great form as Quechee Class with Greg Hills demonstrates

A "Championship Court" was built in the 80s and all the surfaces became Har-Tru. In the mid 1980s tennis was very popular in Quechee. There was a "Quechee Classic" run by Ted MacBeth, a professional. This tournament was timed to precede the Volvo Classic which was run at Stratton Mountain. It attracted many of the world class pros who were to play in the Stratton tournament. There was a pro/am which preceded the Quechee Classic. Around the same time there was a Golf/Tennis Biathlon. Members would be placed in coed teams and would play 9 holes of golf in the morning and sets of tennis in the afternoon.

The Quechee Tennis Classic drew a large and enthusiastic crowd to watch some fine tennis and to raise money for David's House.

David Barrell was chairman of the Tennis Committee in 1981, when plans for a pavilion were presented to the Board. He argued that by building the structure the tennis amenity would be brought up to par with the golf and ski facilities. The membership agreed with his plan, as construction of the pavilion was approved at the May 1981 Annual Meeting.

Twelve months later, the original courts were replaced with Har-Tru (clay) surfaces, which were ready for play by Memorial Day weekend. The 1982 season also introduced the first Pro-Am Tennis Tournament, which teamed Quechee's advanced male players with a selected group of New England Pros.

The first Tennis/Golf Biathlon was held during the summer of 1984, a season which also saw all of the courts in continual play. To meet the demand, the Board agreed to build three additional courts in 1985. The first professional tournament was held the following summer and was called the Quechee Open Tennis Classic. This men's and women's singles competition and Pro-Am became an annual charitable event, and has included many of the top 100 seated pros of both sexes.

A new pavilion was erected in July of 1989 using money from the Capital Improvement Fund. The structure that replaced the recycled information booth used up to that point was larger than its predecessor. An awning covered the observation area, increased in size by 30%, and the Pro Shop doubled its former capacity.

The scope of tennis activities at the Club broadened with the arrival of Chuck Kinyon in 1990. Kinyon, Men's Tennis Coach at Dartmouth College, initiated a training center on the hard courts and created a singles court hitting lane. He was also responsible for the installation of backboards, the acquisition of a new ball machine, and the courts resurfacing. All of the courts saw action during the Thurston Cup Matches in 1991, and in the Mixed Generation Tournament held for the first time that year as well.

Landscaping, repairs, and the construction of a large capacity drain to prevent the courts from flooding were undertaken in the fall of 1992, and completed before the 1993 season began.

One of the most exciting firsts associated with the tennis complex took place in July of 1993. The International Junior Tournament drew competitors under the age of sixteen from Bermuda, Canada, the Caribbean, and New England.

Summer tennis events include a Memorial Day Tournament, adult and junior camps, Kid's Carnival, Independence Day Tournament and Cookout, Singles Tournament, Doubles Tournament, and Mixed Doubles Tournament, Vegas Team challenge and mixers.

Left, top to bottom: 1990 Member and Guest Tournament; 1991 Member and Guest Tournament; Labor Day Scramble - 1990; Travelling Junior Team

The Health Club and Fitness Center

The Quechee Health Club offers a state-of-the-art fitness center with circuit training machines, free weights and cardiovascular equipment as well as an indoor pool and squash court. There is an aerobic studio for group fitness classes, Yoga classes, a youth fitness class, a basic stretching class, a cardio kickboxing class, Pilates classes, stability ball workouts, and an aqua fitness class in the pool. Personal trainers are available to meet individual goals for fitness, rehabilitation, health, or wellness.

Clockwise from top left: Health Club Indoor Pool; Fitness class using stability balls; Strengthening exercises; Fitness Center Treadmills; Squash court; Fitness Center free weights

Aquatics

Before there was a Lake Pinneo, members found relief from the summer heat in a lagoon on the golf course. The refreshing little body of water had its own beach, and was outfitted with a raft.

The Quechee Club Swim Team

The 75-foot outdoor pool was open to the members on July 15, 1972, and was in fact operational long before the construction of the clubhouse began. The fifty-foot indoor pool was available for use once the Clubhouse was dedicated in May of 1974.

Ten years later, the kiddy wading pool was added to the list of aquatic amenities, the direct result of a petition signed by over 200 QLLA families.

The pools have undergone little in the way of refurbishment. The indoor pool did receive a face-lift in 1987 and in 2009. The outdoor pool acquired a heater in 1987, but major renovations did not occur until 1993 when the outdoor pool was repaired, had its lane markers tiled, and in-water lights installed.

Private and group swimming lessons are offered following The American Red Cross Swimming Progressions and advanced courses as well in Lifeguard Training and Water Safety Instruction. The Quechee Club Swim Team welcomes young swimmers 6-18 years of age and of all ability levels providing them an opportunity to take part in Southern Vermont Swim League swim meets.

Left: *Young swimmers at one of the Quechee Club's Swim Meets*

Above: *The Quechee Club pool in earlier days*

Recreational Activities

A new playing field and basketball court has been added near Murphy's Farm. It has been used by the summer camps, both lacrosse and soccer. Basketball and dodge ball tournaments are planned.

The Recreation Department has bounced from one location in the Quechee Club complex to another, and often times back again. It began on the second floor of the Base Lodge. It was created to serve the younger members of the Association and functioned during the early years of the development on a rather limited basis. In the summer of 1974 it offered day care, provided playground and basketball activities, board games, table games, and arts and crafts. By 1975, The Recreation Program had taken possession of the Quechee Fells Barn. The facility was open seven days a week throughout the summer, and broadened its services to include special workshops and classes in archery, ballet and theater. Home to the Recreation Program is once again the second floor of the Base Lodge which is equipped with billiards tables, air hockey, foosball, puzzles and games and a large-screen TV.

Right: *Basketball courts are a popular addition to the amenities offered by The Quechee Club.*

Below: *Pentathlon*

4. The Interim Club used by adults prior to opening the new 1.7 million dollar adult club. Now used as the Young Peoples Club with ping pong and pool tables and other games galore for kids to eighteen years.

The list of the kinds of programs the department offers young people are many and varied: Kids Camps Mini Crew for ages 3-5 and Q Crew for ages 6-12. Kids' Night Out (KNO) offers dinner and activities on scheduled Saturdays during the summer, and bonfires or a movie on Lake Pinneo the nights that KNO is not scheduled.

The Teen Program offers Counselor-in-Training, white water rafting, paintball, zip line, movies and amusement park trips to name a few. Many family events are also scheduled including hiking, canoeing and kayaking. The most popular program enrolling 144 boxes and 200 participants is the February Soap Box Derby.

A juggler performs for a young audience on "Family night" at the Club.

Teen Recreation

Chapter 11

Lake Pinneo

The rumor has been circulating for many years that Lake Pinneo was created because the Quechee Lakes Corporation was being sued for false advertising. The belief was that the development used the word "lakes" plural when in actuality there was only one body of water here fitting that description – Dewey's Pond. It has been suggested that Lake Pinneo became QLC's rebuttal to such allegations. When John Davidson was asked about the validity of such gossip he wholeheartedly denied it, as did Holly Paige. Both men claimed that two lakes were always part of their original plan. Back in the early 1960s, Lake Pinneo was simply called "the second lake," and Dewey's Mill Pond was referred to as the mill pond.

Initially, Davidson had envisioned a 300-acre lake, the level of which would be controlled from an apparatus resting atop the damn in the center of the village. The problems that arose when attempting to make this dream a reality, however, became almost insurmountable. In the end the idea of flooding the land between Murphy Farm and Main Street was abandoned.

Lake Pinneo Is Becoming A Reality

Above is a portion of the new man-made lake at Quechee Lakes Corporation. Taken from the driveway at Ken Murphy's it shows that "Pinneo" is filling up to expectations.

In 1973 D'Appolonia, Inc., of Pittsburgh, PA, was commissioned to draw up a set of engineering plans for a 50-acre recreational lake in an area once known as Gilson Meadow, an area that had been for generations a cornfield. Moulton Construction Company of Lebanon, New Hampshire began executing this design on May 1, 1975.

The Corporation started a campaign to name their new amenity. In a brief article which appeared in the Summer 1975 issue of *The Quechee Times*, readers were invited to submit their suggestions for a name. The winning entry was, since the lake would be open to all Town of Hartford residents, to name it after one of the Town's original proprietors, Daniel Pinneo II. Pinneo served in a number of civic capacities which included Constable, Commissioner of Highways, and Collector. Little else is known about Daniel, except for the fact that he and his family manned the area by the covered bridge during the Revolutionary War, searching for Tories. Their vigilance was rewarded by having the ground they defended referred to as Pinneo's Point.

Construction of the lake took several months and some rethinking. The till which was excavated indicated that something would be needed to seal it, as the soil itself would not hold water. Consultants were called in and they explored a few possibilities, including hauling tons of clay, before settling on lining it with plastic. Sand was poured into the lakebed and then a coat of Polyvinyl Chloride, 20 mil thick, was applied. The 50x60 feet folded sheets, obtained from Water Saver Corporation of Denver, Colorado, were loaded on a "tractor like ladder" and then strategically placed for the twelve-man crew to spread. According to a 1975 Boston Globe account, "...the sheets overlapped about three inches, and were cemented together by hand. On top of this 80,000 cubic yards of fine pond sand were spread one foot deep." The 230,000 yards of soil excavated were used to contour Lakeland golf course.

Lake Pinneo is a popular retreat from the heat

Once the liner was in place, the lake was filled with water "...pumped in at five different points from an underground well located at the lake's north end," according to a Fall 1975 *Quechee Times* report. This method was chosen over using river water for two reasons: state officials were concerned that utilizing the Ottauquechee in this way might negatively impact its flow; and even if allowed, the lake bottom would have to have been much deeper than its six to twelve feet. The process involved in ensuring the latter would have incurred a considerable increase in cost. As it was (and is), the perched lake holds nearly one hundred million gallons of water, and initially took approximately 3,000 pumping hours to fill.

When newly constructed, it was believed that by using water from Pinneo to irrigate both golf courses the lake would be aerated enough to prevent algae growth and general stagnation. Such was not the case. Pinneo had to be closed for a few days in June of 1982 to address the algae buildup. Two years later the QLLA board needed to seek state approval to divert river water into the lake to provide a greater frequency of water change. This was done in hopes of eliminating the spread of algae.

It was suggested, in 1987, that water augmentation was the way to go. During the fall of 1989, a portable diesel pump was employed to siphon water from the river and discharge it directly into the lake. In February of 1990, the lake was drawn down to expose the roots of the aquatic plants in an effort to kill them, and by that summer things were flowing along smoothly once again. They have basically remained that way ever since.

Above: *Lake Pinneo and its long stretch of sandy beach have become a very popular place to spend a hot summer day in Quechee Lakes.*

Chapter 12

QLLA Charities and CHaD (Children's Hospital at Dartmouth)

Quechee Lakes Landowners' Association Charities, Inc. was founded in 1980 by Tom & Ginny Lane as a means for landowners and residents of Quechee Lakes to raise funds for area charities. QLLA Charities, Inc. was incorporated as a non-profit organization on October 8, 1980. Incorporators and members of the Board of Directors were Thomas Lane, Charles Gifford, Michael Baker, James Hutson, and Robert Aker. In 1984 the Board voted to give all funds raised at New England Open Pro Am to CHaD.

The inaugural fundraising venture was the New England Open Pro-Am Golf Tournament. For the first four years, all funds raised at the tournament were divided among four area health care facilities. Then the Board voted to narrow the number of recipients in order to make a greater charitable impact.

Beginning in 1984, all funds raised at the New England Open were earmarked for Dartmouth Hitchcock Medical Center for the benefit of children being treated there. The Intensive Care Nursery and the Pediatric Oncology Department were the earliest beneficiaries. In the last 26 years, QLLA Charities has helped build the only free-standing Pediatric Intensive Care Unit (PICU) in New Hampshire, paid for the QLLA Suite in the Neonatal Intensive Care Nursery, and allowed the hospital to develop, build and run CHaD's PainFree Center, which has become a model for hospitals all over the country. In recent years, funds from the CHaD Classic made it possible for DHMC to build a unique space for pediatric ambulatory care, the CHaD Outpatient Center and the CHaD Family Center.

In the year 2000 the CHaD Classic Golf Tournament provided a profit of $50,000 to a new program known as the CHaD Painfree Children's Hospital Initiative. The theme was "A Night at the Races" betting on horse racing on a large screen TV and two auctions, a silent and open auction.

In 2003, the CHaD Gala was added on the Saturday night prior to the Monday golf tournament. This festive social event has not only provided a venue for non-golfers to participate for

a good cause, but also has dramatically stepped up the dollars raised for the children.

In 2005, QLLA Charities started an endowment to support the Child Advocacy and Protection Program (CAPP) at CHaD. This program reaches out to the area's most vulnerable children – those who have been neglected or physically, mentally, or sexually abused. With a team of physicians, nurse practitioners, social workers and child life specialists, the program works in partnership with local police, prosecutors, schools, medical care providers, courts, social workers and service agencies to help support children and their families during this very challenging process.

In addition, the program focuses on educational and prevention efforts to keep children safe from harm.

Since its founding, QLLA Charities has donated $1.57 million to assist the dedicated staff at CHAD in providing the most up-to-date medical care to sick and injured children in our region.

From 2000 to 2001, CHaD classics funds supported the development of CHaD's pain free program created to reduce pain and stress for children who need to go through some tests and procedures. This program has become nationally know for its effectiveness and outstanding compassionate care for children

CHaD CLASSIC
CHILDREN'S HOSPITAL
Dartmouth-Hitchcock
Gala
Presented by
Quechee Lakes Landowners Association (QLLA) Charities, Inc.

From 2002 to 2005, tournament proceeds help construct CHaD's outpatient center that opened in July 2005. This remarkable facility offers a child-friendly interactive waiting area and pediatric center that brings together all of CHaD's pediatric and surgical subspecialties.

From 2006 to the present, QLLA charities has made a five-year commitment to support one of CHaD's most fragile and vulnerable patient populations – abused and neglected children – through a pledge to provide operating as well as endowment funding for the child advocacy and protection program (CAPP).

This year, 2010, QLLA Charities will celebrate 30 years of generous support of Children's Hospital at Dartmouth.

In the year 2000 the CHaD Classic Golf Tournament provided a profit of $50,000 to a new program known as the CHaD Painfree Children's Hospital Initiative. The theme was "A Night at the Races" betting on horse racing on a large screen TV and two auctions, a silent and open auction.

Koala Quilt

Hole in One prizes and donors: Quarter Horse offered by Barbara West, two $25,000 checks by Drew Cunningham, a Ford Taurus by Allen Hall for Gateway Motors

Above and left: *CHaD Gala Banquet*
Below left: *CHaD Registration 2010*

Chapter 13

Woodstock and Hanover

Quechee village is ideally situated between Woodstock, Vermont and Hanover, New Hampshire, less than ten miles to reach either historic town. By its close proximity to these towns, Quechee has been able to benefit from their sophistication and their wide variety of cultural offerings as well as restaurants, shopping, and community events.

Woodstock was settled in 1761 and was originally the seat of Windsor County. Many of the lovely homes are considered among the finest examples of early American architecture. Just off the village green is a covered bridge over the Ottauquechee River which winds its way through the heart of town. Three local churches have steeple bells cast by Paul Revere or his descendents. The Rockefeller family has bought land and restored the Marsh-Billings Estate, now a national park. The Marsh-Billings-Rockefeller National Historical Park is the only national park to tell the story of conservation history and the evolving nature of land stewardship in America. The boyhood home of George Perkins Marsh, one of America's first conservationists, and later the home of Frederick Billings, the property was given to the American people by its most recent owners, Laurance S. and Mary F. Rockefeller.

*Above - Marsh-Billings Mansion; **Right** - Woodstock Historical Society*
***Below left** - Woodstock Covered Bridge; **Below right** - Woodstock Inn*

Just twenty minutes from Quechee in the opposite direction lies the charming historic community of Hanover. The town has a population of 10,850 and is the home of Dartmouth College, which was established in 1769. It is the educational, medical and cultural center of northern New England. Hopkins Center for the Arts houses galleries, concert halls and theaters. Dartmouth Medical School is the fourth oldest in the country and Dartmouth-Hitchcock Medical Center is a teaching hospital and regional referral center for the National Cancer Center. It offers broad interdisciplinary programs in biomedical research, education, patient care and service.

Every semester The Institute for Lifelong Learning at Dartmouth (ILEAD), founded in 1990, offers many continuing learning opportunities—courses, forums, lectures and travel programs to area residents and members.

Below, clockwise from left - Dartmouth 1874 historic building; entrance to Hood Museum of Art, Dartmouth Library; Wilson Hall, a performing arts facility; Hopkins Center for the Arts

Chapter 14

Murphy Farm

Over the years Murphy Farm has been called Whittlesey-Newton Farm, Gilson Farm, Sybilholme Farm, and Merrydale Farm.

At one time it was 200 acres and said to be the second oldest house in the valley, dating from 1780.

In 1919 John and Abba Fancy lived there with their young family. The gable end of the long narrow house they occupied faced the Ottauquechee River and the upstairs rooms of the structure were barely six and one half feet high. In 1928, Eleanor and Charles St. George purchased the property and the oldest landmark in Grafton, NH, known as the old Buffum place. The latter, which they moved to Quechee and attached to the existing farmhouse that same year, was erected by Moses Leavitt in 1725.

Top: *an aerial view of Murphy Farm*
Above: *Murphy Farmhouse in the fall*

The St. Georges were also responsible for adding the dormers and building the large barn to hold their herd of Jersey cows. A Fitzgibbons by birth, Eleanor St. George was a descendant of one of Ireland's prominent ruling families, and an author of some merit. Albert and Dottie Schaal purchased the property from St. George in 1952 to raise Guernseys. They called the property Merrydale. For over a decade they cultivated it: planting the fields, tending to cows, chickens, and pigs, sugaring, and raising a family. Yet, hard work and dedication were not enough to sustain the farm operation. The family had to supplement its income by utilizing the gravel pit on the property.

Top: *Murphy Farm in winter*
Above: *A Garden Club luncheon held at Murphy Farm*

Ken Murphy obtained the farm in 1965, concentrating most of his efforts on the gravel pit operation. In 1968, he sold half of his holdings to the Corporation.

In February 1987 a General Agreement was presented to the QLLA membership agreeing to buy the Murphy Farm property from the Quechee Lakes Corporation, approximately 4.5 acres for $750,000. QLLA purchased Murphy Farm from QLC in 1987. The Landowners' were approached by an outside party interested in obtaining the property in 1989, but it was ultimately decided that the house would be renovated. By using moneys from the Capital Improvement Fund supported by QLC contributions made at the initial sale of any development property, the membership was spared any additional financial burden the incurred by such an undertaking.

Phase one of the renovation process began in 1989. The house was brought up to code, a heating system was installed, the wiring was upgraded, and the fireplaces were refurbished. In 1991, the Food and Beverage Service began offering a Sunday brunch and the menu was soon expanded to include weekend dinners. Though dining, except for special QLLA events, is no longer offered on weekends, during the 2005-2006 renovation of the clubhouse, Murphy Farm was used for all member dining.

This quaint New England farmhouse with the charming atmosphere of a country inn nestled on the shores of Lake Pinneo is now available for private, catered parties and there is plenty of room for a large tent on the grounds. For a few years in this decade musicians gathered here with banjos, guitars, fiddles, harps, and dulcimers. It was a time for anyone to join in or just stop by and listen and enjoy.

Chapter 15

Marshland Farm and The Quechee Inn

Colonel Joseph Marsh arrived at the mouth of the White River amidst the Land Grant controversies in 1772 along with two brothers, two cousins, a widowed mother and ten of his twelve children. Between Joseph and his brother Able, the two Marshs owned almost all of the land along the north side of the Ottauquechee in what was to become known as the Village of Quechee. In 1778, he was appointed Vermont's first lieutenant governor serving under Governor Thomas Chittenden.

In 1793, at the age of sixty-seven, Marsh built a home "...opposite where the Quechee River breaks into little islands." Once completed, the Georgian style home was referred to by the locals as the Baronial Mansion. Marsh conducted all of his business from his new home, including overseeing the sawmill, gristmills, and fulling mills erected near the falls.

The Quechee Inn through the years

Above: circa 1975;
Right: Summer 2010

When Marsh died in 1811, the farm was left to his son Daniel and approximately 500 acres transferred to the Honorable John Porter, another prominent resident of the village, who then became the owner of Marshland, the home and farm from 1846 to 1901. He was, during his life in Quechee, one of the original stockholders in the Woodstock Railroad; President of the Ottauquechee Savings Bank; Director of the Vermont/Canada Railroad; member of both the state legislature and senate; Director of the Vermont State Prison; Commissioner to prepare and erect the State Capitol in Montpelier after a fire destroyed the existing one in 1857; and Probate Court Judge for 36 years.

The farm changed hands many times and there were many new owners over the next 70 years. They grew corn and wheat and raised livestock on the farm. When John Davidson came to Quechee, he purchased the farm and 400 acres and Marshland was converted to a 17-room inn in 1975 by the Quechee Lakes Corporation and subsequently sold with five and a half acres to Michael and Barbara Yaroschuk in 1978. The Yaroschuks made many renovations, adding eight guest rooms, a commercial kitchen and dining room. Wilderness Trails located at the back of the property offers kayak trips, cross-country skiing, fly fishing instruction, mountain biking, and canoeing.

The Quechee Inn is today a well-known landmark in the village and guests come from all over the United States to enjoy its traditional ambiance, fine restaurant and recreational activities.

Top: *The view of Dewey's Pond across from The Quechee Inn*

Center: *A wedding party arrives by hot air balloon for the ceremony held at The Quechee Inn*

Bottom: *Adjacent to The Quechee Inn is a field owned by Quechee Lakes Landowners' Association.*

Chapter 16

The Quechee Village Green

The one thing Quechee did not have, besides lakes, when the Corporation first came to town was a quintessential Village Green. But, like the lakes, the developers saw the potential for creating it, and set about to do so. Designs were quickly drawn for a public park, a playground and a common, complete with historic buildings on a 20-acre meadow between the river and Main Street.

Both the Ottauquechee Regional Planning and Development Commission and the Upper Valley Planning and Development Council endorsed the final plan, released on May 1, 1973. Al Moulton, then Executive Vice-President of QLC, said when he announced the project, "We have become increasingly aware of the village's need for a public park open to all, and we think this plan is the answer. It provides something for the kids as well as the adult members of the community."

What it offered was a baseball diamond, free play area, a playground, park benches, and a walkway along the river in a 15-acre section that would retain the open state of the flood plain. It also included a common dressed with five century homes imported for this purpose on a five-acre span above the surrounding plain. Carol Dewey Davidson recalls that John had a vision of these historic houses surrounding the Village Green. He located them, had them disassembled and shipped to Quechee, carefully numbered piece by piece and stacked along the green. Unfortunately, soon after the Kane Financial Corporation and the Quechee Lakes Corporation became a subsidiary of CNA Financial in 1971, the dismantled homes were taken away and disposed of.

The Village Green took two years to complete, and was finished on July 1, 1975 and conveyed to QLLA in 1977 with the provision that it be be available for public use. An easement was provided for access for Hartford residents. Today its is owned by QLLA and jointly maintained by the Town of Hartford Parks and Recreation and QLLA.

Clockwise from top left: *The Quechee Village Green Playground; The Village Green and athletic fields; the Village Green during the annual Hot Air Balloon Festival; The bandstand erected in 1985*

A bandstand was added to the center of what would have been the common area in 1985. The bandstand provides the perfect setting for Quechee folk to gather on summer evenings and hear local bands perform.

By mutual agreement the Hartford Department of Parks and Recreation and the Quechee Club maintain the park and the Green.

A Memorial Walk was added to the green during the summer of 1992. This joint effort between the Quechee Garden Club and the Association was undertaken to honor members of the community who have died. The Quechee Club's maintenance staff constructed phase one of the project, a gravel path running the length of the western side of the green. The Garden Club paid for all of the necessary materials, and the QLLA crew the labor.

The Village Green is enjoyed by the membership and the public alike. The event that the Green has become most noted for is the annual Hot Air Balloon Festival and Crafts Fair, sponsored by the Quechee Chamber of Commerce since 1979.

Barbara Yaroschuk with Michael's mother, Kathy and Chris Yaroschuk and Charles Jameson at the dedication on the Quechee green.

Chapter 17

Polo Field

Polly West of Quechee rides with the Quechee Polo team enjoying their 16th season with a winning record. Riding hard left to right. West, Jennifer Howe and Dr.Steve Roberts. Watch them Saturdays at 2 p.m. at the Polo Field.

Choat began organizing the team. The site selected off Dewey's Mills road was the only one of adequate level terrain with Quechee Lakes boundaries. In the months which followed, a playing surface together with sideline parking areas and a lead-in road were cleared of late fall hay and corn stubbles. Players were recruited from horsemen in nearby towns and the Quechee Polo Club was incorporated. From the outset the club was fortunate to draw on the coaching expertise of Dr. Stephen J. Roberts, one of the nation's foremost authorities on polo. An inductee in the athlete's Hall of Fame as an undergraduate polo star, he had coached Cornell's great intercollegiate polo team for 25 years.

Another QLLA property that receives considerable use and is often available to the public is Dewey's Flats, more commonly known as the Polo Field. Once sprouting hay and corn, this meadow became home to Quechee's very own polo team in 1974.

That year landowner and former QLLA President, Robert Tuttle, asked the corporate powers that be to consider the introduction of the game to the area. Arguing that the "Sport of Kings" had indeed become dominated by "America's adventuresome middle class," and would therefore align itself nicely with the Corporation's current amenity package, Tuttle petitioned for the free use of an as yet to be determined bit of QLLA common land. He also assured them that the team would function as an autonomous unit and make no further demands on the Association.

The old corn and hay field was allocated for the use of the Polo Club, and as it was being prepared for play, Tuttle, veterinarian Dr. Stephen Roberts, and Woodstock resident Allyn

Quechee played its first match July 5, 1975 before a crowd of 800 people, defeating a hard-riding Sugar Bush Polo Club 5-2 on a field so dusty that players often lost sight of long hit balls. Since then the field has been

graded and periodically seeded, aerified, and fertilized so that its turf is thick and easily withstands the pounding of horses' hoofs.

In 1981, the Quechee Polo Club was accepted for membership in the prestigious United States Polo Association and allowed women to join its ranks on Dewey's Flats the same year. The team, consisting of six to eight players from central Vermont and New Hampshire, plays about 12 games a season, six of these are "away." When at home, however, they can be found galloping

Above: *The 1973 Scottish Festival in Quechee gets underway with a parade down Main Street. Featuring the pipes and drums of the Granite State Pipe Band and the Wee McGregors, the parade wound down Main Street and through the covered bridge.*

Bagpipes turned out in force for the Scottish Festival at Quechee.

their way across the impeccably groomed field, (tended to by the Quechee Club golf maintenance crew) on weekend afternoons during the summer months. Games are scheduled each summer by Joe Kozlik, the Quechee Polo Club president, with teams throughout New England and upstate New York.

The Vermont Symphony Orchestra holds an annual Upper Valley concert every summer which is very popular. Also, every August the Polo Field is home to the Scottish Festival featuring music, dance, games and food.

Chapter 18

Special Olympics

"Let me win, but if I cannot win, let me be brave in the attempt."

The Winter Games literally grew out of the Winter Carnivals held in Quechee, and in other towns and villages like it across the nation. In 1975, Vermont and Maine pioneered the Special Olympic Winter Games concept by incorporating snow-related activities into their Special Olympics programs. Quechee was the Vermont site where this historic event took place. The premiere games were more closely related to a winter carnival in nature, and, in fact, were often labeled as such in succeeding years. These early events were not officially sanctioned by individual sport governing bodies, nor were the participants professionally trained, but neither the lack of endorsement, nor the want of experience hindered the 300 1975 participants from enthusiastically engaging in tubing races, slide derbies, and snowshoeing exercises.

By 1977, 600 Special Olympians, wearing borrowed or donated equipment, skied, skated, and snow-shoed their way to personal victory on the Clubhouse grounds.

In 1978, 38 states had added Winter Sports to their rosters and Vermont's endeavors continued to flourish. That year Quechee hosted 650 Olympians and 250 volunteers from throughout the state. By 1979, the numbers grew to an amazing 800 participants and 400 volunteers. Due to the huge success of the Winter Carnivals, two sites were chosen for the 1980 festivities, Quechee, and Duxbury, Vermont.

In 1981, the focus of the Special Olympics Winter Sports Program changed. The one-day event that had provided a score of activities was transformed into a two-day, sanctioned, skiing and skating competition. Participants became trained athletes, and coaches became certified instructors. In March 1992, the Special Olympics Winter Games came to Quechee.

Two hundred athletes representing 18 teams from Vermont were greeted at the Quechee Club by volunteers and host families on February 28, 1992. Opening ceremonies were held February 29 with Governor Howard Dean presiding over the festivities. Hundreds of spectators cheered the athletes as they marched toward the stage to John Williams Olympic fanfare theme. The Olympic Torch was lit. They recited the special Olympic oath "Let me win, but if I cannot win, let me be brave in the attempt." Those athletes qualifying earned a place to compete in the World Special Olympics in Austria in March of 1993. Over 300 people volunteered their time and energy, and many their homes, to make it a reality. After the rigorous one and one half days of competition, the athletes celebrated their success at a dance held in their honor at the Clubhouse.

In 2000 Quechee again hosted the winter games. It was a qualifying event for the 2001 Special Olympics International Winter Games in Anchorage, Alaska. The Special Olympics

Flame of Hope lit the cauldron in Quechee. The athletes competed in alpine and cross country skiing, figure skating and speed skating. Simon and Pia Pearce's son David competed in many events. Pia Pearce was very supportive in fundraising for the Vermont Special Olympics, "Our athletes are lucky to come back to Quechee year after year. They are comfortable with where things are and how the event works. We are grateful to everyone who makes this event happen. As athletes build strength, skills and coordination, they are also building confidence, social skills and self-esteem."

It takes the participation of the whole community, hundreds of volunteers to host the games. Quechee volunteers organized an Olympic Town, a place for athletes to relax after participating in

activities. There were sports clinics and, of course, at the Quechee Clubhouse, entertainment, awards ceremonies and presentations and a dance party which was greatly enjoyed by the athletes. Schools donated facilities and their students served breakfasts and dinners. Supplying food involved huge numbers – 1400 slices of bread for sandwiches, 200 pounds of potatoes, 90 dozen eggs, cases of fruit, thousands of brownies and cookies, hundreds of burgers, truckloads of water. One of the major challenges was to find 400 rooms for athletes and coaches. Hundreds of athletes, family members, coaches and volunteers were housed either by host families or in donated homes and for many, lasting friendships were made. Ken Lallier and his QLLA staff took care of the snow shoe and cross country venues and Dave Courtney, the ski patrol director, set and ran the alpine events. Many volunteers were ski escorts, place judges, timers, stagers, sandwich makers, bus drivers, and most importantly, applauded and cheered for the athletes.

After 2000 the Special Olympics felt they should change venues to rotate around to different geographic areas of the state. The hope was that the Special Olympics would come back to Quechee every third year but unfortunately that plan never came to fruition.

Opposite: It takes a village—the Village of Quechee and surrounding areas—to help put on the Winter Special Olympics.

Left: A Special Olympics Athlete with his coach

Above: A proud Special Olympics athlete displays his medals.

Chapter 19

Quechee Condominiums and Homes

The great diversity of condominiums and homes owned by our 1,392 members attests to the appeal of Quechee Lakes.

Kingswood

Newton Village

Coach Road

Lakeland Village

Landmark

Mill Run

Quechee Hollow

Greensway

Snow Village

Fox Hollow

Deere Run

The Ridge

Saltbox

Sugar Hill

Sugar Hill

Birchwood

The Vale

Above: *A rear view of Birchwood Condominium, designed in the traditional New England row-house style. Birchwood was the first condominium built in Quechee Lakes.*

Windsor Village

Dartmouth Place

Homes within Quechee Lakes offer scenic views as well as convenient locations to local amenities and attractions. Architectural styles are many and varied—traditional, log cabin, contemporary, and deck homes.

Chapter 20

QLLA Volunteers Build the Ottaquechee Trail

The village of Quechee is historic and picturesque, featuring fields, hills, woods, a pond, waterfalls, a covered bridge, a lake, and, of course, the centerpiece, the Ottauquechee River —a perfect setting for a pleasant walk or hike, yet no trail has existed in the past and unfortunately visitors' and residents' cars continue to traverse Quechee's narrow roads to see the village "sites."

For many years a concerned group of QLLA members has been interested in establishing a walking/hiking trail through the village of Quechee, but through the efforts of Sheila Armen and the Community Affairs Committee of the Quechee Lakes Landowners' Association (QLLA) the Ottauquechee Trail plan has finally come to fruition. The original pathways project has become Friends of the Ottauquechee Trail, Inc. (F.O.O.T.), now established as a volunteer organization in the State of Vermont.

The much needed walking path, named the Ottauquechee Trail, is being created by QLLA volunteers along the QLLA polo field and QLLA hay field next to the Quechee Inn. Eventually it will continue along the river to the village and the clubhouse.

OTTAUQUECHEE TRAIL

Lake Pinneo

Dewey's Pond

TRAIL HEAD

WEST

EAST

QUECHEE, VERMONT

Top: *Map of the Ottaquechee Trail*

Above and opposite: *QLLA members turn out to help build the trail.*

Appendix

Quechee Lakes Landowners' Association Presidents

QLLA Board Presidents

Name	Term of Office
Hollis S. Paige	1970-1972
Robert W. Tuttle	1972-1974
Elbert G. Moulton	1974-1977
Donald A. Gannon	1976-1977
Frederick Callowhill	1977-1978
John O'Brien	1978
John M. Gallaway	1978-1979
Charles Gifford	1979-1980
David Marshall	1980-1981
Olof T. Dormsjo	1981-1984
William Raitt	1984-1986
Robert Neilson	1986-1987
J. Ronald Hutcheson	1987-1988
Leslie A. Ide	1988-1989
Robert Stambaugh	1989-1990
Walter L. Sullivan	1990-1991
William P. Emerson	1991-1992
James J. Von Gal	1992-1994
John Gibb	1994-1996
Carol Moser	1996-1998
Len Berliner	1998-2001
William Craig	2001-2002
Joe Noonburg	2002-2005
Patt Taylor	2005-2007
Bruce Macdonald	2007-2008
Ted York	2008–2013

Tennis Champions 2002 - 2010

2002	Ian Arvin
2003	Alex Hirshberg, Suzy Bottaro
2004	Bob Hickey, Heidi Schultz
2005	Bob Hickey, Janine Tabas
2006	Mike Duseau, Karen Hartley
2007	Mike Duseau, Emilia Hodel
2008	Mike Duseau, Karen Hartley
2009	Rod Hartley, Karen Hartley
2010	John Lunny, Olivier Barbier

Golf Champions 1972 - 2010

	MEN	WOMEN
1972	Bill Goldbach	
1973	Joe Hayes III	Jean Talmage
1974	Bill Purcell	Ruth Katz
1975	Bill Purcell	Ruth Katz
1976	Bill Purcell	Jean Talmage
1977	George Grimm	Jerry Russell
1978	Bill Purcell	Jean Talmage
1979	Jack Hatcher, Jr	Jean Talmage
1980	Ed Holland	Ruth Katz
1981	Bill Pursell	Nancy Guerin
1982	Bill Pursell	Nancy Guerin
1983	Donald Brief	Nancy Guerin
1984	Chester Davis	Nancy Guerin
1985	Terry Deleo	Nancy Guerin
1986	Kerry McNamara	Nancy Guerin
1987	Terry Deleo	Nancy Guerin
1988	Terry Deleo	Mary Lou Ketchum
1989	Kerry McNamara	Sue Chmieleski
1990	Rod Beebe	Chris Wilder
1991	Rod Beebe	Nancy Guerin
1992	Terry Deleo	Sue Chmieleski
1993	Terry Deleo	Rene Leoni
1994	Terry Deleo	Nancy Guerin
1995	Mike Fox	Chris Wilder
1996	Rod Beebe	Rita Kennedy
1997	Jim Keighley	Kathy Hansen
1998	Ned Waters	Sue Norton
1999	Dave Murray	Carol Dawson
2000	Jim Keighley	Lisa Lacasse
2001	Jim Keighley	Kathy Hansen
2002	Ned Waters	Rita Kennedy
2003	Jim Keighley	Michelle Marcus
2004	Ned Waters	Carol Dawson
2005	Mike Nesseralla	Pat Decaire
2006	Ned Waters	Lisa Lacasse
2007	Jim Keighley	Pat Decaire
2008	Jim Keighley	Shelley Yusko
2009	Bill Dwyer, Jr.	Sarah Clunan
2010	William Dwyer	Pat Decaire